ISLETA PAINTINGS

"Old man bear is waiting for his time to come, waiting over at the hills west side of plaza, he will be alone, he has bear hand skin on both hand and eagle wing feathers. He is holding prayer stick which he will place when he comes to hold in middle of dance plaza. When he comes in village he makes all kinds of noise . . . then he run east, north, west, south, in middle he places prayer feather."

ISLETA PAINTINGS

With Introduction and Commentary

by

ELSIE CLEWS PARSONS

Edited by

Esther S. Goldfrank

SMITHSONIAN INSTITUTION

WASHINGTON, D. C.

1962

BUREAU OF AMERICAN ETHNOLOGY
Bulletin 181

To

ESTHER S. GOLDFRANK *and* JULIAN H. STEWARD

to whom I owe the opening of Isleta

FOREWORD

For over two decades, and more than any other person, Dr. Elsie Clews Parsons influenced the course of ethnological research in the Pueblos of the Southwest. She began her investigations in Zuni in 1915, and until shortly before her death in 1941 she made frequent visits to the "living" Pueblos, both western and eastern, indefatigably and meticulously collecting comparative data on their social and ceremonial life. Her scientific enthusiasm drew many of her colleagues to the area (preeminently Dr. Franz Boas to the Keres); and her generosity, spiritual no less than financial, permitted many a young student to become an independent—and sometimes controversial—observer of Pueblo society.

As Dr. Parsons indicates in her Introduction, information on the Pueblos is not easy to come by, for all aspects of Pueblo life are highly ceremonialized and under priestly direction. Among them the Eastern Pueblos were least responsive to inquiry. Isleta has been no exception.

In the fall of 1925 Dr. Parsons asked me to "crack" Isleta in one month! After 9 days of frustration, I found one man willing to talk, but our meetings were made so difficult by members of the community that we were forced to continue them in Albuquerque, 13 miles away. Six months later, Dr. Parsons returned to the Southwest and to the investigation of Isleta. Except for a Laguna immigrant, her major contact was with the one man I had worked with previously. It was primarily on the basis of her interviews with him, also conducted outside the Pueblo, that she wrote her "Isleta, New Mexico," which was published in the 47th Annual Report of the Bureau of American Ethnology.

In 1936 a copy of this Report came to the notice of an Isletan townsman. In a letter, forwarded to Dr. Parsons by Dr. Julian H. Steward, then with the Bureau of American Ethnology, he expressed his approval of the text, but criticized the lack of illustrations. And he said he could—and for a price he would—remedy this deficiency.

Any anthropologist who has worked in the Pueblos could forgivably be skeptical of such intentions. But Dr. Parsons, whatever her doubts, had the curiosity and the imagination—those essential adjuncts of successful scientific investigation—to tell him to go ahead. In 5 years the artist, who in compliance with his own request will remain nameless, sent Dr. Parsons well over 100 watercolors of extraordinary interest and beauty.

In a memorandum, dated September 1941, Dr. Parsons writes: "Pictures and Commentary and Introduction in order." This is why I have made no radical changes in her manuscript. However, for greater ease in reading, I have incorporated in her Commentary the "captions" originally placed under the pictures, and where the pictures were not available at the time of printing, I have included elsewhere relevant excerpts from the accompanying Commentary. I have also added a few footnotes which carry my initials and I have placed between brackets my remarks inserted in the text (remarks in brackets in the quotations are Dr. Parsons'). I have not sought to make the spelling or capitalization in the quotations consistent, nor have I italicized any Indian or Spanish words in them, preferring to permit the artist's transcriptions to stand as he made them. But I have italicized the first use of non-English words in Dr. Parsons' observations. Finally, I have included among the references certain relevant publications that have appeared since her death.

Needless to say, after a delay of 20 years, it is a great satisfaction to know that these paintings will now become available not only to scientists and artists and those who have felt the enchantment of the Southwest, but to all who want to understand another people and another way of life. Many persons and institutions have made this possible. I should like to thank the American Philosophical Society for permitting the use of these paintings and Mr. René d'Harnoncourt, director of the Museum of Modern Art, for housing them while they were in New York and for his efforts to find support for their publication. He, like Dr. Parsons, hoped they would all appear in color, but the great cost ruled out this desirable mode of presentation. I am most grateful to the Bollingen Foundation for making it possible to print a few of the pictures in color and thus give a better realization of the artist's range and personality. I also want to thank the Bureau of American Ethnology, particularly Dr. Matthew W. Stirling (the former director), who so quickly understood the extraordinary value of these paintings, and Dr. Frank H. H. Roberts, Jr. (the present director), and Mr. Paul H. Oehser, chief of the Smithsonian Institution's Editorial and Publications Division, who have been so helpful in getting this volume into print. Mr. Frank Dobias was of greatest assistance in matters of design, and Mrs. Eloise B. Edelen handled the endless editorial details with patience and ingenuity. My deepest gratitude goes to Dr. Elsie Clews Parsons and the nameless Indian artist to whom we owe these remarkable "Isleta Paintings."

Esther S. Goldfrank.

New York, N. Y.
April 8, 1960.

CONTENTS

LIST OF PAINTINGS

XV

xvi

INTRODUCTION

Isleta is a town of the southern Tiwa, Tanoan-speaking Pueblo Indians on the Rio Grande about 13 miles south of Albuquerque, N. Mex. The population numbers around 1,200 persons. All houses have one story, some with Spanish portico, and there is a large plaza, rather poorly defined, which the townspeople still refer to as "laplaza." On the north side stands the Catholic church with its high-walled grounds. Orchards and fields surround the town and its suburb toward the railway, about half a mile to the west.

This suburb, Oraibi, was settled about 1880 by a small group of Laguna immigrants, Pueblo Indians also, but speaking Keresan, a language entirely different from that of their hosts. Why the settlement is called Oraibi, the name of a Hopi Indian town in Arizona, no one seems to know, but this name may well be connected with the Isletans' return in 1718 from their long visit to the Hopi. Although the Isletans did not participate in the great Pueblo Rebellion of 1680, at the time of the reconquest they had already abandoned their town and were seeking refuge from the Spaniards in the safe Northwest.

A description of Isleta is included in the 47th Annual Report of the Bureau of American Ethnology (Parsons, 1932). A copy of this publication came into the hands of an Isletan townsman, and in 1936 he wrote to the Bureau:

I have read the magazine printed by Washington in 1932. The history is true and exact, but the pictures to complete it are missing. I have drawn some of them. . . .

These drawings you will never see anywhere because no one [else] could do them, it is too hard. They are afraid to die if they do them. I don't want any soul to know as long as I live that I have drawn these pictures. I want good satisfaction because they are valuable and worth it. They [the subjects of the pictures] are most secret. No one can see them but Indians who believe.

I have no way of making a living, no farm. . . . If I had some way to get help in this world I would never have done this. I expect to get good help.

Felipe (this is not his true name) did get help. And over a number of years he delivered the paintings reproduced here. His remarks penciled on them have been incorporated in the captions and commentary [cf. Foreword]. His letters, in which relevant matters are explained and elaborated, are on file for the interested student.[1]

---

[1] At the American Philosophical Society, Philadelphia, together with the originals of the paintings and Dr. Parsons' other papers.—ESG.

1

Felipe's apprehensiveness about being found out was expressed in almost every letter. It was wholly sincere, I think, even when it was translated into pecuniary terms. Fear has to be compensated for, as another Pueblo Indian once put it when he asked me "How much will you pay me for my fear?"

Felipe writes:

I will send the pictures a few at a time as long as you promise me you will keep me away from trouble. I will complete all the secret drawings. It will be all right for you to publish them some day, but don't tell who did this, it [would be] hard on me. I will look for mail soon; write before I change my mind about giving you the drawings.

Pueblo Indians are trained from earliest childhood to keep the major part of their life hidden from their White neighbors and visitors. It is an intelligent technique of self-protection against those who for various reasons would make changes in Indian culture. This motivation for secrecy, however, is more or less covert and unanalyzed, but it fits in with the characteristic and deep-rooted Indian attitude that religious knowledge and ritual, when divulged to the noninitiated, lose their potency. Just as a prayer or medicine depreciates when imparted, so the life of the Pueblo will be impaired if outsiders know about it. Besides, the life of the informer is endangered, magically and practically. Felipe, however, was willing to take a chance. "I am not afraid of sickness or dying. I am ready to die any time as long as I have a little good time with this little money."

Of moral scruples in our terms there are a few expressions. After referring to offerings to the dead made on the ash piles, Felipe writes: "I don't know if I am doing right to tell all this or not. Sometimes I feel funny." Again, "If I had not seen the History [the Bureau publication] I would not give you or anybody any drawings." This appears to be the familiar rationalization for telling a secret—"You know it anyway." It is also an illustration of the general attitude of the Pueblo Indian who tells you something only when in his opinion you know enough to understand.

Felipe is a school-taught Indian, and he may have had some practice in drawing at school. His work shows no influence, however, from the American Studio, as do pictures from the upper Rio Grande Pueblos. Unlike Sante Fe, Albuquerque is not an artist's haunt. Taken chronologically [the dates the artist wrote on the paintings are placed at the end of the accompanying commentary], Felipe's pictures themselves indicate that he is largely self-taught, and this has intriguing implications for the problem of personal esthetic development. However, in this volume the order dictated by the subjects represented seemed to be more important.

Felipe's pictures have been compared with early Persian compositions, and, I am told, they have no little esthetic appeal. That they have considerable ethnographic

2

value, I know. Many details are given that could hardly be brought out in verbal descriptions or in photographs, which, in any case, are taboo in Isleta. To no ceremonial, except the Saint's Day celebrations, are White people admitted, and from certain performances, Indians not members of the group engaged are also excluded. That the discussions of ceremonies given in the Bureau Report are far from complete is evident from the accompanying commentary.

The written notes contributed by Felipe I believe to be trustworthy. And fortunately he rarely feels called upon to paraphrase his information in order to make the Indian aspect intelligible to a White person. He seems to think that, although the published "History" needed correction and amplification, it was written from the Indian point of view. Let me confess that I enjoy the compliment, the greatest indeed that an ethnographer can receive.

Except in the introductory and concluding sections, I have followed the annual ceremonial cycle in presenting these pictures. But it should be remembered that as a young man an Isletan would go on a communal rabbit drive, would hunt deer, join in dances and races, play the clown, fetch ritual spruce from the mountains, and serve as a guard on a Saint's Day. As he grew older he would, almost surely, assume a more important place in curing, hunting, and safeguarding the town; and he might become a medicine man, hunt chief, or war chief. No one man would hold all these offices or perform all these tasks, but every townsman would know a great deal about them. In the pictures we see older and younger men functioning together. We see children taken into the ceremonial chamber so that they may know "where they belong" and young girls called upon for ritualistic services.

In Isleta the life of women generally is played down because the ceremonial life is played up, and here women have only minor roles. Of their daily secular life we have no pictures, although I asked for them. Activities, such as cooking, eating, sleeping, or the merely economic aspects of farming, hunting, and handicraft, did not appeal to the artist as subjects for portrayal—and this in itself is significant. Certainly it underlines the well-known difficulty of securing Pueblo autobiographies. As Dr. Leslie White has written, efforts to obtain them result in little more than reports of ritualistic experiences.

In this respect the pictures of childbirth are peculiarly revealing, for the ritualistic aspects are emphasized and midwife and doctor are as important as mother and child. The functioning of the medicine man at this time is, by the way, a comparatively recent innovation. Formerly midwives still learned their profession from one another, either informally or through an apprenticeship. "Same as the medicine man," writes Felipe, "an old lady taught them." Her name was Cecilia Chavez.

3

"She died, and Ana Lupe and Juana Dominga Zuni were left. Ana Lupe died; Juana Dominga was left. Juana Dominga taught only because no one offered herself." When Juana Dominga died, they had no one.

Then old man Rey Zuni, Chief of the Town Fathers [there are two groups of medicine men, Town Fathers and Laguna Fathers] and old man Sun, Chief of the Laguna Fathers, talked it over and decided to appoint specialists. Rey Zuni called his helpers together; they agreed and so he chose Perfecta Anzara or Keipop [a woman member or "mother" of the Town Fathers] and as her helper Bautista Zuni [nephew, first assistant, and successor of Rey Zuni]. Then Rey Zuni called for a ceremonial and called together all the people. Early before sunrise they had the ceremonial [installation?]. Rey Zuni preached to the people telling them: "Our great father and mother looked around and saw that there was no one to look after childbirth, and they decided to appoint someone, so our great father put his hand on the heart of Keipop [mother spreading] and appointed her, and to be her helper, Bautista Zuni. From now on you will know whom to call when an angel is coming to live on this earth." Then all the people called out "hewiau! hewiau! thanks! thanks!" When Rey Zuni died in 1925 and Bautista Zuni became Chief, Bautista appointed Creancio Carpio as childbirth helper. The Laguna Fathers never appointed anyone; any Laguna Father goes when one is called for.

As most of the pictures deal with ritualistic aspects of Isleta life, I shall briefly review the town's ceremonial organization and calendar.[2]

Like other Pueblo Indian towns, Isleta has a Town Chief and a War Chief (Kumpa), the latter, who is also head of the War or Snake Society (Kumpawithlawen), being more or less the executive of the Town Chief. The Town Chief has still another warlike executive, the Bow Chief [3] (Kabew'iride), who succeeds to the office of Town Chief.[4]

Dual organization is further emphasized by the presence of the so-called Black Eye and Red Eye moieties. Their officers direct clowning, hunting, and ball playing, and are prominent in the irrigation ritual and certain maskless kachina dances. Everyone in the Pueblo belongs to one or the other of these moieties.

And everyone also belongs to one of the seven Corn groups that hold winter and summer ceremonies for the Sun—winter and summer solstice ceremonies we have called them, perhaps mistakenly, for they occur well before the solstices and, according to available information, no solar observations are made at these times.

---

[2] For a fuller statement, consult Parsons, 1932, 1939.

[3] At Santo Domingo the Town Chief had two very important associates, one of whom was called Bow Chief (White, 1943, p. 305, note 2).

[4] Elaborating on this point, Felipe has written: "Sun-Arrow was Town Chief, died some time ago, and Dolores Jojola was assistant to Town Chief; he was Kabewhiride. Next to Kabewhiride is Kuampa. Old man Remijo Lucero was Kuampa." And again in the same letter: "Town Chief's name was Sun-Arrow, died, then Kabewheride took his place, and when Kabewheride died then Kuampa took his place." See also commentaries on Paintings 25 and 87, and page 8, note 7.—ESG.

4

A person belongs to his mother's Corn group, and in sickness or at death his Corn Chief (he may be referred to either as Corn Father or Corn Mother) serves as an intermediary with the doctors or expediter of the deceased. In the Pueblos such functions often adhere to clans, but the Corn groups at Isleta are not exogamous— a person may marry inside or outside his group indifferently—and they therefore cannot be considered true clans. In fact the Corn Fathers and their helpers, the directors of the group in charge of its ceremonial, operate as a priesthood. At least two of the Corn Fathers or Chiefs are in control of the maskless kachina dances.

There are also two groups of medicine men who are both curers and weather makers: the Town Fathers and the Laguna Fathers. And there is a Hunt Chief.

Secular officers—Governor and war captains—are appointed annually in accordance with the prevailing Spanish-Pueblo system. They hold Spanish canes of office and the head war captain is known as War Chief of the Cane. He and his aides have ceremonial as well as secular functions.

As might be inferred from an organization so complex, the annual round of ceremonies, Indian and Catholic (there is a resident Catholic priest at Isleta), is quite full and the ceremonies are well distributed over the year. In December, there are the Corn group ceremonies, which approximate solstice ceremonies, and Christmas; in January, there is Kings' Day;[5] in February, there are *Thliwa* (maskless kachina) dances for snow and rainfall, and a general cleansing ceremony for the people, land, and houses by the medicine men or shamans, this followed by the irrigation or ditch-opening ceremonial and initiations into the medicine societies. (Felipe writes on February 1, 1941: "They will make one new medicine man as soon as kikewaie Baleyo, our Lady [mother] Moon comes in full clear the first of this month.") In the spring, ritual races are run and "every five years," i.e., sporadically, there is a scalp ceremony. The major celebrations for the saints occur in June (for San Juan on the 24th and for San Pedro on the 29th, with cock racing and snatching) and in August (for San Agostín, the patron saint of the Pueblo, on the 28th, with image and flag being carried through the fields). On June 15, at the close of the rain rituals by the Corn groups, there is a Thliwa dance, and at the end of September, there is a Thliwa harvest ceremony. On November 1 and 2, rituals for the dead are observed.

The cult of the dead is both Spanish and Indian. Weather and crop spirits (Thliwa) live on the mountains, like the weather and season spirits of the western Keres, and, like the kachina elsewhere, they are impersonated in dances; but at Isleta

---

[5] This is primarily celebrated by the Laguna colonists, although Isletans take some part in it.

5

no masks are worn. Also, as elsewhere, the medicine men get their powers from animal spirits.

The cosmic spirits are Sun, Moon, Lightning, Wind, Earth, and Fire. Among western Keres there is a collective term for the more powerful cosmic spirits—*kopishtaiya*—and to this term or concept corresponds, I surmise, the Tiwa term *Weide* (pl. *wenin*) which includes the mountain or moisture spirits (Thliwa) and which has proved quite as baffling to define as kopishtaiya. To the Pueblo Indian almost all nature is invested with spirits; to western Keres and southern Tiwa some of the potent and general nature spirits—not plant or animal spirits, the earth, or the common dead—are collectively kopishtaiya or wenin.

Felipe identifies Sun with Weide, and he also refers to the moisture spirits (rain and snow), the Thliwa (compare Keresan *Shiwana*), as Weide, "our father rain" or "our rain god." This is one of his few paraphrases. Unfortunately it does not clear up other uses of the perplexing term, which is often employed as if it were a term for a high god.

Other Isletans have also equated Weide and rain. But Felipe does make one new rain spirit identification—a very significant one. The stillborn or infants dying before baptism become rainmakers. This explains why food offerings and prayer sticks are carried to their hillside grave cairns by members of the Corn groups (see Parsons, 1932, pp. 299 f.). By excluding the unbaptized from consecrated ground the Church may have inspired their recognition as a special class of spirits in the Indian pantheon. A similar phenomenon appears to have occurred among the Catholicized Andean Indians of Ecuador.

Also in other respects Felipe's paintings and letters give much new and enlightening data on the pantheon and ceremonial organization. In addition they correct earlier misinformation, light up obscurities, and amplify meager statements in the Bureau Report. In the following discussion I have italicized new and significant contributions.

We learn that there is *only one Round House*, not two such kivas, and that although the Round House is used for Thliwa (maskless kachina dances), for "making" or painting the moiety *kapyo* clowns, and for race ritual, it is primarily the place where the scalps are kept and where offerings are made to the enemies, the "Navaho," from whom the scalps were taken. In other words, the Round House is the Scalp House. *Its manager is the permanent War Chief* (Kumpa). This has an important comparative implication. The Isleta Round House was borrowed from the Keres not earlier than the 18th century, for there is no record of such a building when Isleta was visited and reported on as an abandoned town in 1717. This was

6

just before the townspeople returned from their visit of 17 years to the Hopi. Perhaps the round kivas of the Keres that were used for kachina dances served also as Scalp Houses. The moiety clowns of the Keres, as well as the Tewa and Tiwa clowns, have military traits, and Keresan clowns use the Round Houses.

The clowns at Isleta, as elsewhere, are associated with the Thliwa or kachina. The Isletan Thliwa chiefs, the *Chakaben, are appointed by moiety,* as are the temporary kapyo clowns and the permanent grandfather clowns. Only the moiety chiefs may paint the impersonation of *Aiyayaode,* who is nearer to being a full-fledged kachina than any other Isletan impersonation. The *moiety organizations are in control of the Thliwa cult* or a major part of it.

The dances of the anthropomorphic mountain-dwelling rain spirits of the Pueblos, the kachina, are performed with mask and without mask. No Tiwa, Sandía Tiwa excepted, use masks in the cult, nor is the cult as highly developed among them as in other Pueblos.

At Isleta, there is no kachina organization proper, no general Kachina cult into which all the youths are initiated; but there are kachina or Thliwa chiefs, the Chakaben, whose head *is also the Chief of the Yellow Corn group.*[6] Besides, as we have noted, the moiety chiefs function at Thliwa dances, also the clowning moiety "grandfathers" and the kapyo clowns, quite as in the Kachina cult elsewhere.

There appears to be one more association between moieties and moisture: It is the function of the moiety chiefs to carry to their special cemetery the dead infants who are prospective rainmakers.

Of interest also is the *assignment of little girls as "mothers"* to the moiety organization. The moiety chiefs "came up without mothers," as Felipe puts it, i.e., in their militant past there was no need for females, but later, after coming in contact with others, they learned to "make mothers." As such groups as Corn groups and Medicine societies had "mothers," only a bit of involutionary patterning was necessary.

As noted above, the Chief of the permanent War Society, the Kumpawithlawen, is referred to as Kumpa. His insignia are bow and arrows *which are called "black cane" because Kumpa himself is called Black Cane, Tuefuni.* I will refer to him as War Chief and to the other members of his Society, of whom there are four, as war chiefs or members of the War Society. War Chief and members of the War Society

---

[6] The Yellow Corn or Yellow Earth People are said to have lived across the river where a few houses are still occupied. These people were "mean people" and spoke a little differently. Here are supposed to have dwelt the Isletans who migrated to Isleta del Sur. This suggests that another and distinct Tiwa group once consolidated with the people of Isleta—the first mention of Pueblo masks, by the way, by the Conquistadores is a reference to masks seen among the southern Tiwa in 1582 during the Espejo expedition.

7

are vowed in sickness, and tenure is for life. At installation each new member is given the bow and arrows insignia. *Kumpa is thought of as representing the personage "who gave the first living people bow and arrows for hunting and war."*

The War Chief is referred to as "elder brother" to the head of the annually elected war captains. *War Chief of the Cane, Cane Chief, or Tuewithlawe,* himself annually elected, is the head of these captains. All the war captains carry canes of office, and may be called Cane Chief. The War Chief of the Cane is from the Black Eye, or *Shifun,* Moiety and he appoints five Black Eyes from different Corn groups as war captains. He also appoints a Red Eye, or *Shure,* Moiety assistant, who in turn appoints five men from his moiety. Thus there are two head war captains or War Chiefs of the Cane, and 10 other captains—a group of 12. The group's function is to guard all ceremonies, dances, and races, and to assemble people "because the War Society [the permanent organization] *"may not go after people."*

This point and others in the above account clear up inconsistencies in the Bureau Report with respect to the relations between the two War groups which, largely because of terminology, were ambiguously described by earlier informants. That the permanent War Chief was called "Black Cane" and the annually appointed war captains had canes of office and might be called Cane Chief was a peculiar source of confusion.[7]

The punitive function of the War Society represented in Painting 103, the punishment of the circle, and *the religious source or aspect* of this physical penalty, familiar elsewhere,[8] is explained for the first time, at least for Isleta.

Particularly valuable are the pictures of the rain ceremony of the Laguna Medicine Society. The rain ceremonies and dances of the Keresan medicine societies have been lapsing, giving way, so to speak, to the rain dances of the kachina in the ascendant Kachina cult. But at Isleta the Thliwa cult, the maskless Kachina cult, is less assertive and the medicine men's dances persist.

At Isleta neither the scalps nor the dead, i.e., the adult dead, have a rainmaking function, as in other Pueblos. Since offerings are made to the dead they must be

---

[7] The source of confusion is more than terminological. It is important in this connection to remember that since the death of the last "real" Town Chief (Sun-Arrow or Domingo Juipe) in the eighties, radical changes are said to have occurred in the pattern of succession. There is considerable evidence that one Kumpa, instead of installing a new Town Chief, assumed this office permanently himself. The interested reader will find additional information on these matters in Parsons (1932, p. 256, note 45, and p. 259, notes 67 and 68) and in French (1948, pp. 13 ff.), which brings together data collected in 1942, a year after Dr. Parsons died.—ESG.

[8] Cochiti (Dumarest, 1919, p. 173); Santo Domingo (White, 1935, pp. 23 f.).

expected to be of use to the living, but in what way is not clear, unless the deceased had "power" as a medicine man or as a Corn Chief who "returns to the Sun whence he came," or as an infant who, dying before baptism, *becomes a rainmaker.* However this may be, ghosts are far from welcome. Here, as in other Pueblos, they are exorcised 4 days after death, but in Isleta an additional rite of exorcism is previously performed at the grave. The corpse, after being covered with a layer of soil, *is pounded with a heavy piece of wood, a ritual pestle.* No such practice has been reported elsewhere in the Southwest. Nevertheless, it suggests Apache influence. The southern Athapascans, Apache and Navaho, have a very acute fear of the dead and of ghosts.

Considerable information on ritual practice and concept is contributed by Felipe. We learn that cleaving feather against feather, a common curing technique among Pueblos, is done so that Wind may carry sickness away. The feathers are eagle feathers, the shaman's feathers. *Duck feathers are markedly associated with the Corn groups,* which would of itself indicate that these groups had rain and crop interests and some association at least with the Thliwa or moisture spirits, and thus with the Kachina cult.[9]

And the Corn groups do have such associations. Yellow Corn Chief, as noted, is Chief of the Kachina cult, Chakabede; *Shichu* Corn Chief is in charge of a Thliwa dance group. In fact the relations between the Isleta Corn groups and Thliwa or wenin is not very different, conceptually or ritually, from that between the Zuni paramount Corn or Rain chiefs (the *Ashiwanni* of the Directions) and the Kachina cult.[10]

Something about pigments, as well as feathers, characteristic of the ceremonial groups can be gleaned from the pictures (cf. Paintings 22, 64, 65). Apparently face and body painting is more important among the Tiwa and Keres than among the Zuni or Hopi. For instance, we learn from Felipe that the Chief of the Laguna Fathers is painted with a bear paw design and other members of the Society with a lightning design, which is significant of the twofold functions of the medicine men—curing, Bear being the curing patron, and weather control. The Town Fathers, however, are not painted.[11]

---

[9] In the kachina prayer sticks of Zuni and Laguna, a duck feather is conspicuous.

[10] The Kachina cult of the Pueblos seems to be an overlay on the old Thliwa (Taos-Isleta)-Shiwana (Keres-Zuni)-*Okuwa* (Tewa) cult, the cult of Mountain, Rain, or Cloud spirits, a farflung cult of ideology among the highland peoples of America.

[11] Prof. Edward P. Dozier, himself of Pueblo descent, has in a personal communication commented on the fact that, contrary to his experience elsewhere, certain ceremonialists in the kiva are shown in the pictures fully clothed (cf., among others, Paintings 33, 54, 67). In all probability this is a more or less recent innovation in Isleta.—ESG.

The association between the Yellow Corn people and ritual fire making is new information, as is the description of their slow match of cedar. This is the first time among the Pueblos, as far as I know, that fire is said to be associated with the directions.

Through Painting 33 we learn about the Salt Circle, although not why it is so called. It lies in the house of the Town Chief and is the most sacred of all ritual objects and complexes. Here in a central pit in a buckskin bag are contained the "lives" of all important creatures including the townspeople.[12]

Information about the pit or bag was given in connection with a tragic happening. According to Felipe, when the White Corn Chief died in 1940, the bag could not be found. The White Corn Chief died on December 17, during his ceremony, after he had fasted 3 days, without eating or drinking. Before he died he made a lightning mark on one of his medicine water bowls in his private ceremonial room. After he died, the assistant Corn mother found the mark on the bowl. He must have known he was going to the end. A few days later the Shichu Corn chief, Bautista Juancho went to the Town chief's house to get his road, [that is] permission to begin his fasting, to perform his ceremony (napei)—he always has to be the last of the Corn chiefs to start his ceremony. When he went to the Town chief's house with his assistant, he found that the nest (ekue) was gone, missing from the hole where it had been kept for many years. In that nest (ekue) the bag made of deerskin was placed. That is where they ask for their health. They believe that White Corn chief hid that away or stole it. When that nest was lost, the people of the Corn groups were all worried and excited. They said their life was gone. Then they all gathered in the War chief's house. All the Corn chiefs and assistants asked the War chief to take pollen [corn meal] to the Town chief to ask our great medicine chief [chief of the Town Fathers?] for his light look [crystal?] from our Mother Moonlight to find the nest. I will finish the story of what happened next time.

(The rest of the story was never sent. Inferably, *Moon is the patron spirit in divining for lost things.*)

For some time before they welcomed the Laguna immigrants, Isletans may have been on visiting terms at Acoma and Laguna. They probably passed through Laguna on their way back from Hopiland after the reconquest. One of the Isletan medicine societies is called Laguna Fathers, its "mother" or patron being younger "sister" to the "mother" of the other society, the Town Fathers. ("Father" is the usual Isleta reference for any ceremonialist.) Both societies are Keresan in character, getting power through their corn fetish "mother" and through the supernatural animals. The only difference, but an important one, is that the Isletan society, although includ-

---

[12] At Acoma in a secret room in the Town Chief's house there was an "altar" in charge of *Tshraikatsi,* who was one of the two associates of the Town Chief and who had more supernatural power than the *cacique,* for he "worked" to increase the supply of plants and game (White, 1943, p. 2). Probably the counterpart of this chief at Isleta was *Haukabede* (cf. Paintings 129–132).

10

ing specialists, is itself less specialized than the Keresan society. This difference may well indicate that Tiwan and indeed Tanoan society is and was less highly ceremonialized, less socialized, if you will, than Keresan society.

The Town Fathers and the Laguna Fathers are groups of shamans with individual powers like shaman assemblages of northern tribes. Such shamans tend to have individual patrons, and there are a few hints at Isleta that this is the case. Lightning is a patron, or shall we say "power," and Moon, "Our Mother Moonlight," is the "power" of the medicine men who find lost objects, the detective shamans. The outstanding patron of the Town Fathers is Eagle; of the Laguna Fathers, Bear.

However long established in Isleta these medicine societies may be, it is a matter of record that certain innovations were introduced by the 1880 Laguna immigrants, among whom were several medicine men. The most outstanding was Juan Rey Sheride or Churina. His daughter, Juanita, a midwife, introduced the use of the badger paw at childbirth[13] (Painting 1). Juan Rey himself introduced stick swallowing and the cure for ant sickness, and he decorated the walls of the ceremonial chamber of the Laguna Fathers with the spirits of the pantheon. (Seemingly, *frescoes were in vogue at Laguna, probably in the kivas* that were torn down at the time of the row which led to the emigration to Isleta.) The walls of the chamber of the Town Fathers are undecorated.

Juan Rey Sheride did not get on well with Pablo Abeita, the White Corn Chief, and ultimately Juan Rey left Isleta and with his daughter went to live at Sandía where he soon died (in 1923) "because he broke his promise to do his ceremony at Isleta." No doubt the clash between Juan Rey and Pablo Abeita was one between two strong personalities, but it also points to ceremonial rivalry probably of long standing between the Corn groups and the intrusive Keresan societies.

The southern Tiwa were among the first Pueblos to be subjected to Spanish penetration. Isleta was founded late,[14] whether by southern or by northern Tiwa[15]

---

[13] The mother of Juanita Churina was the daughter of José, the Shiwanna medicine man of Laguna and, according to Felipe, Juanita got the badger hand "midwife" ritual from her grandfather who, I have no doubt, learned it from someone of Hopi descent. (It seems to me that Juanita may have been taught midwifery by her mother who used to return to Laguna to assist old José in ceremonial. Note that through this family there was a close ceremonial connection for years between Isleta and Laguna.) Juanita died "a few years ago" at Sandía, where she left "badger hand." The ritual lapsed at Isleta when Juanita went to Sandía about 1922. So Felipe drew in the badger hand to add ritualistic richness to the picture.

[14] How long the present site of Isleta has been occupied is a moot question which may not be answered until the middens, the sacred "ash piles," are dug into. As yet at Isleta Dr. H. P. Mera has found only two sherds of the glaze-paint pottery that was common in the Rio Grande area prior to 1700, and these may well have been carried, he writes me, from settlements to the south. He is dubious about early settlement.

[15] It is a tenable hypothesis through pottery evidence and the reconstruction of ceremonial history that after the burning of old Taos, say in 1650 (H. P. Mera), some of the people of Taos founded Isleta, possibly becoming neighbors, as suggested, to a settlement of southern Tiwa.

is uncertain, but, in either case, Spanish contacts have left many marks on its culture. I realized this in my first study, and now Felipe has contributed more data along this line of acculturation in childbirth, baptismal, funerary, and memorial practices. St. Christopher and the Virgin are called upon in labor; defective infants are "cured" by contact with a domestic animal freshly slaughtered; Catholic ritual is conspicuous in naming infants, in paying vows, in religious processions and church dancing, and in shrouding and burying the dead, whether infants or adults.

In certain of these loans the process of acculturation is exceedingly interesting. In some cases, while both Indian and Spanish rites are resorted to, they are kept distinct, as in painting the deceased and shrouding the body in a friar's habit, or in burying food in the grave and leaving it on top of the grave, or in considering the deceased infant if unbaptized a rainmaker and if baptized a little angel. In other cases these different rites are well integrated, as in the kinsman's prayer at the grave, when the deceased medicine man is prayed to and given a candle just as a saint would be given a candle, or as in covering mirrors during storm or curing lest lightning shatter the house or the conservative temper of the doctor be affronted. For long I have been intrigued by the resemblance between the Catholic kiss of adoration and breath rites which have a wide distribution among Indians. Painting 50 clearly reveals the union.

There are a few cases of apparently accidental resemblance as in ritual spitting, or in the use of the five-pointed star or the cross, which to the Catholic is an amulet, but to the Pueblo a summons to the spirits of the directions. Here we may consider the calendrical adjustment to Catholic ceremonies as a purely practical arrangement. If the winter solar ceremonies were true solstice ceremonies, they may have been moved back in the calendar to make place for the Christmas celebration which seems fuller at Isleta than in any other Pueblo. At Taos there is the same calendrical shift, and it is also made at Laguna where we know that the dislocated ceremonies were winter solstice ceremonies.

As I have given a full bibliography for all the major subjects and much of the detail covered by these pictures in the Bureau Report (1932) and in "Pueblo Indian Religion" (1939), I have included few bibliographical references here.

Finally, I wish to thank Prof. George L. Trager for his work on the annotated glossary, which appears at the end of this volume. The transliterations of Indian words in the commentary are my original recordings.

12

COMMENTARY AND
PAINTINGS

BIRTH

PAINTING 1

Summoned by the chief of the Corn group to whom the prospective mother belongs, the childbirth doctor and midwife are attending the woman who is sitting on a sheep pelt. With a stone implement *(koata)* the doctor is about to "whip" the woman on her back "to loosen the baby." From his stone-using function this specialist is called *koatamide.*

In the early stone implements there is magic power. If you tap a deer on the head with a koata he will drop dead. Arrow points are held in the hand (cf. Painting 11) or in the mouth, carried in the belt, or laid on altars, against witchcraft.

On the ground lie the doctor's two eagle feathers—eagle feathers also have power—his pouch of sacred cornmeal, and a badger paw, "Old Woman Badger's hand." Badger digs out quickly, and on this occasion, as in Hopi practice, I believe that the paw is passed down the body of the woman to speed the delivery. This is an instance of the sympathetic magic common among Pueblos, particularly in child bearing and during infancy.

July 28, 1937

14

Birth

WOMAN ASSISTANT

Stone whip he uses to loosing baby

Doctor
childbirth Specialist

page 214

Woman

sleepskins

Old woman Badgers hand.

medicine bag

no 1

PAINTING 2

A Catholic spirit may be called upon in childbirth, in this case San Kietiano (Saint Christopher?) who is the "master of childbirth and of nothing else." When labor begins the painted wooden tablet is brought into the house and placed on an altar table. The midwife or "Childbirth Woman" sits alongside.

The tablet is about 13 inches square and 1 inch thick. It has been freshly painted by a Mexican. "They have used this saint a long, long time, as you can see from the way the corners have been bitten away."

"San Kietiano does not belong in the church. He was brought long ago from Las Lente. In Isleta he was in the house of Grandma Cecile [Cecilia Padilla, midwife]. When one of the family died another one took the saint. [The tablet passed on within the family.] At present the saint is at the house of Lady Carlota Lujan."

Los Lentiles, once a Tiwa town called Rainbow Village, is about 5 miles south of Isleta. It is largely Mexicanized, but Isletans still go there to pray to another privately kept saint, San Gonselito, and to dance for him.

At Zuni and Jemez, and probably in other Pueblos, there are saints that "do not belong to the church."

February 1, 1941

16

no 2.

PAINTING 3

"When a woman has pain, sick for day, having trouble in childbirth, to heal her from pain she bites at the saint, using one corner where it has been bitten into." A bowl of medicine is at hand "to get heat into the body."

The midwife "is praying, begging the saint to keep them and pass them through this trouble." At this time, too, vows may be made to the Virgin (cf. Paintings 46, 50).

"After 4 days [the confinement period] they take the saint back to the private house where they got him, with song and prayer and church-bell ringing. When they hear this the people are glad and give thanks to San Kietiano that the lady came out all right."

February 1, 1941

18

No 3

PAINTING 4

After the umbilical cord is cut and tied the midwife burns the end of a corncob and, as it smoulders, applies it to the severed end of the cord. The mother is not allowed to look on.

For 4 days, in the morning, a special powdered clay is applied.

June 23, 1941

PAINTING 5

After the midwife has burned the cord and washed the infant, the doctor "gives the baby to be child of all the directions," orientating him in his world, in the spirit world, by pointing his head in each of the five ritual directions—east, north, west, south, and for the fifth direction, up, down, and middle (cf. Painting 9). The up-down-middle motion is made at the south point in the imaginary diagram.

Many sacred objects are motioned ritualistically toward the directions by the Pueblos. Spirits are associated with the directions: rain, animal, and corn spirits, among others.

July 28, 1937

22

Assistant woman

Doctor

south   up

East   down   west

north

M 2

PAINTING 6

When they are ready to leave, doctor and midwife receive food in pay "for their trouble." As seen in the picture, ritual food fees or gifts are commonly placed in a line in front of the recipient (cf. Painting 13). On this occasion soup has been put in the nearest bowl, bread in the large bowls, peaches in the small bowls.

July 28, 1937

24

Doctor.

Doctor women assistant.

Bread

Soup

Soup. Peaches Bowl.

Reciving Their Gift. After. Ready to leave.

no 3.

PAINTING 7

After the 4-day confinement, early in the morning, the mother, carrying the baby, circles four times around a freshly placed pot containing coals of fire in the middle of the room, and steps over the pot in order "to take sickness away." While this rite of exorcism is being performed, the infant's "aunt" stands by, waiting to bathe the mother and take her, with the infant, to the plain in the east at sunrise. Note the mother's pallet and the tub and yucca roots for the bath.

Fire Old Woman is a member of the spirit pantheon in Isleta as in Cochiti, Nambé, and Zuni. Also, among the Keres a fire is kept up during confinement against witches who cause sickness.

July 14, 1939

page 215

Crossing over fire

Aunt waiting to go out
to hand east who is person
coming to name the infant

bed

Fire?

bath tub

water wat

Child birth

not.

PAINTING 8

The "aunt" is casting meal from her basket to the Sun, and in his presence she is giving the baby the name which will be confirmed later by the Chief of the Corn group. The sacred meal is held between thumb and index finger.

Mother and "aunt" are giving thanks to the Sun that the mother came through all right. They are asking the Sun to give the infant a long life, the fervent and recurrent prayer of all Pueblos.

Thanking the spirits, the chiefs, and one another for ritual or formalized services is a common Pueblo practice. There is no thanking for casual service.

Naming an infant at sunrise, "showing the baby to the Sun," is also general among the Pueblos, and the "aunt," the father's sister or other kinswoman, is customarily the godmother.

July 14, 1939

28

meal

meal Basket

Out side facing east where the sun is coming out praying.
Given the baby name before the sun

No 2

PAINTING 9

At the close of the winter ceremony of the seven Corn groups, members of each group enter their respective ceremonial chambers to be given a sip of medicine water (Felipe calls it "holy water") "in order to live happily and long." At this time, too, an infant born during the year is brought in to get his "Corn name." By this name he will be recognized by the Sun after he dies and directed on his road to and under Sunrise Lake.

Here the Corn Group Chief is naming the infant, showing him to the sacred ears of corn lying on the ground altar. The corn is yellow, indicating that the group is Yellow Corn.

Is the timing of this baptism modeled upon the church practice of christening after the Mass? There are other Catholic forms. The chief sprinkles the infant from the medicine bowl, and makes the sign of the cross on his forehead, each palm, each sole. The godmother takes home some of the medicine water.

January 15, 1936

Figure 11.

PAINTING 10

The doctor is putting the infant into a cow's stomach still warm from butchering, and uncleansed. This treatment appears to derive from European folk medicine.

Many cures are carried out at home, as among all the Pueblos. An offering of a little cornmeal wrapped in cornhusk accompanies the request to serve, and the doctor is asked for home treatment, I believe, by the Chief of the Corn group to which the patient belongs.

January 15, 1940

PAINTING 11

This man offended the ants by pouring oil on an ant hill and setting it afire. The ants entered his body and were eating his eyes. For 4 nights in the patient's house the Ant Father, one of the specialists in the medicine societies, has put up his altar: his "Mother" or corn fetish and his stone arrow points. Each night with his eagle feathers he brushes the ants from the patient's body. For a fuller account, see Parsons, 1932, pages 443–444.

In this cure, as in others, the medicine man holds in his hand a stone point, ever an amulet against danger.

Ants may have some helpful function—as they have at Zuni, in war—for any Isletan leaving town may sprinkle crumbs for them. "They say Ant is the best man to think things out" (ibid., p. 383, note 77, p. 384, note 78).

November 1936

34

34 Juan and his arts. page 443.

PAINTING 12

A 4-night cure for a witch-sent sickness—in this instance a rag and "bad thoughts" have been "sent" into the woman's body.

Among all the Pueblos, witches send all sorts of injurious things—cactus thorns, bone splinters, sticks, glass, pebbles, ants, and an unidentified insect described as looking like a headless centipede. Witches are envious people or people who feel aggrieved. They can change into animals or birds and can transform others. They have the powers of medicine men but they work evil only. Curing is for the most part against witchcraft.

On the first night, represented here, one doctor is pulling from his mouth a rag which he has sucked out of the patient and which he will place on the ashes behind (note that only one foot of the patient has been bared). The second doctor, cleaving one eagle feather against the other, is "cleaning with feathers," giving all "bad thoughts" to "Wind to carry away." This is the first interpretation of this rite of exorcism, so common among the Pueblos, that I know of. Wind Old Woman may herself cause disease, and so, in accordance with the Pueblo way of thinking, she can also cure it.

In this treatment, as is usual in private curing, the doctors have not been painted. The Corn Group Chief, who has asked for this ceremony for his "daughter," sits near the bowl of tobacco and cornhusk.

January 23, 1939

36

Corn Chief, his ask for this Ceremonaly for his Clan daughter

getting rags for mouth

Cleaning with feather

Tobaces

sick woman

placing old rags on ashes

shoe off
left side

shoe off

For slight sickness Cure for 4 nights at private home

PAINTING 13

The fourth night the patient's relatives offer food to the doctors and through them to Weide. All pray and tell Weide the woman must get well and live to be old. They will help the doctors carry the food home.

January 23, 1939

38

medicine man

PAINTING 14

The offering is being made at the home of the Medicine Society Chief in his private room. The Corn Chief is asking the Medicine Chief to give a sweat bath at the river to a "daughter" of his Corn group.

Note how the medicine man keeps his things: bandoleer and pouch of cornmeal, bear-claw necklace, crystal, gourd rattle, bear paw, eagle feathers, medicine bowl, and, within the table drawer, his Corn Mother fetish.

Among all the Pueblos cornmeal, coarsely ground, is cast or sprinkled in prayer, in asking the spirits for something. This is the use the medicine man will make of the cornmeal given him by the person requesting his ceremony.

The medicine man wears a bear-claw necklace, and over his left hand he will draw on a bear paw because he gets power from Bear, the curer animal.

The crystal, pendant from the necklace, gives a vision of anything happening anywhere—crystal gazing for second sight, inferably through the power of Moon (see Introduction, p. 10).

With his gourd rattle the medicine man will accompany his songs. Songs are the most important and most secret part of his ritual.

The prescription for medicine water is also very secret. The medicine is sprinkled in the directions or on persons or given them to drink or take home.

In the medicine bowl, stone fetishes are immersed, and their in-dwelling beings are summoned by song or whistle.

May 16, 1939

40

Bird necklace

wakan kabade

hereonhere he keep his mother

Medicine man

meal on tumback Bundle & big little quinte me kinnade

Receiving message from their own Clan daughter for sweat bath at River

This here they keep their things in their private home in sepeat room

PAINTING 15

Steaming under a blanket is practiced in other Pueblos, but not regular sweat bathing, which is common among Athapascan and Plains Indians. The Isletan sweat house is or was a tipi type of Navaho shelter. Inferably, Isletans borrowed the practice originally from tipi dwellers, probably Mescalero Apache, although they compare it today with Navaho usage. Analogously the scalps kept at Isleta (cf. Painting 97) are called "Navaho" scalps, but they may have been from Mescalero Apache who raided the Isletans. "Navaho" means merely "enemy."

The sweat "hogan" is made of clay "like an oven," writes Felipe, that is, clay and straw cover the poles except where they project through the top. This hybrid structure used to stand near the river, but after the old medicine men who knew about the cure died, it was destroyed. "They still know how, but since White people have begun to come around to watch, they hide from them."

This sweat bath cure is taken only in summer. It is "given to one with rheumatism or bone ache or with skin diseases."

April 18, 1939

42

sweat Bath hogan made of Clay like oven

PAINTING 16

Inside the sweat house the Medicine Chief is dipping out his decoction to pour over the hot stones to make steam. ("The water is fixed with roots, it has power.") The Chief and his helper will sing four songs. "By the last song you feel like crying from the heat. Water pours from your body, your mouth is dry. After the fourth song you run out crying and jump into the water. They do all this near the river so they will cool off quickly."

Plains Indians also jumped into the water.

May 16, 1939

PAINTING 17

The patient is taken out before sunrise. The Medicine Chief leads her "by the tips of his feathers"—the usual ritualistic way. He is warning her to have good thoughts because "our Mother, Fire Old Woman is mean, she might burn your life out." The patient is "thinking of Fire Old Woman, asking her to be kind to her daughter." This form of curing is "the hardest of all to get by" (endure).

May 16, 1939

46

No 3.

Pointing to woman on may
telling her she must have fought longest
This hardest burning togt fry.

The woman pointing of Oldmothepine asking to be kind to his slaughter

PAINTING 18

Navaho scalps are kept in the kiva built like the Keresan kivas and generally called the Round House. The woman is being led by the medicine man to the pit behind the firescreen(?) to feed the scalps. The man hiding behind the post will make a noise and touch her on the back to scare her as she passes by. She will believe it is a dead Navaho.

I was once told of a man who ventured alone to feed the scalps but became so frightened that before he got halfway down the ladder he just threw his meal offering away and fled, telling his brother who was waiting for him that his toothache was gone. "He was cured because he was frightened."

I was also told of a Spanish cure for toothache, or rather a Spanish-Indian cure. A girl took a candle out to the western hill for her deceased kinsman (cf. Painting 135), the Snake Father in the Laguna Medicine Society. He was very powerful. Within the hour her toothache was gone.

Since the scalps cure toothache, they may, consistent with the Pueblo point of view, be thought to cause it; and inferably, sickness from fright is cured by fright. Among the Spanish Mexicans fright, *espanto,* is a common cause of sickness.

April 18, 1939

48

women with Tooth ake

hiding where his not seen
to Touch the women
from the ⟨⟩ she ⟨⟩
⟨⟩ scard ⟨⟩
get ⟨⟩

Dark they do this curing at night only.
In Round house.

no 2. pl. ⟨⟩
17

PAINTING 19

Before the corpse is placed in the middle of the floor the mirrors are turned to the wall. This is Spanish and quite general European folk practice, but Isletans have extended it and integrated it into their own conceptualizations.

The mirrors are also turned when it is about to rain or storm.

"When the rain comes with storm or lightning the lady of the house comes running and turns all the mirrors face to wall. If she did not do this our father Lightning would come in, they claim, because he likes to look into the glass and would come in and shine more fire. He is big, does not fit into the house and would bust the house."

Again, when they have medicine men in the house to doctor the sick, they turn or cover or take down the mirrors. "The doctors do not want to see themselves when they pull rags out of their mouth."

A month later Felipe wrote, "Indians never used to have mirrors. They never knew how they looked. When you White people made mirrors then we learned how we looked. That is why our father Rain (kikawe Weide) doesn't want us to have mirrors and with lightning and thunder would come and bust the house." Like many people, Pueblos and others, Felipe indulges in contradictory interpretations.

February 1, 1940

PAINTING 20

The "aunt," to the left of the deceased, and the other woman are awaiting permission to wash his hair and dress him. Note water bowl and twig brush.

In death, as in sickness, the Chief of the Corn group a person belongs to is sent for. He will make the "road" for the deceased "to go to the Sun from whom he came" and 4 days later, after the burial and the 4-day period of mourning, he will destroy the "road," shutting the ghost off from returning.

Among all Pueblos, making the road to altar, shrine, or any place to which the spirits are summoned is an important rite. The road may also be made for brides (Hopi, Acoma), and it may be closed against supernaturals or enemies, as happened at Hawikuh against Estevan, the Moor, who discovered the Pueblos, and against that captain of Coronado who was driven from Acoma.

June 20, 1939

52

page 248 in History

PAINTING 21

The "aunt" will also wash the face of the corpse. Then the water will be thrown inside the threshold, probably because, if disposed of outside, it would be dangerous to others. The bowl will be broken, the pieces also left inside the threshold.

Among the Pueblos similar death services are always performed by paternal kinswomen.

May 18, 1937

54

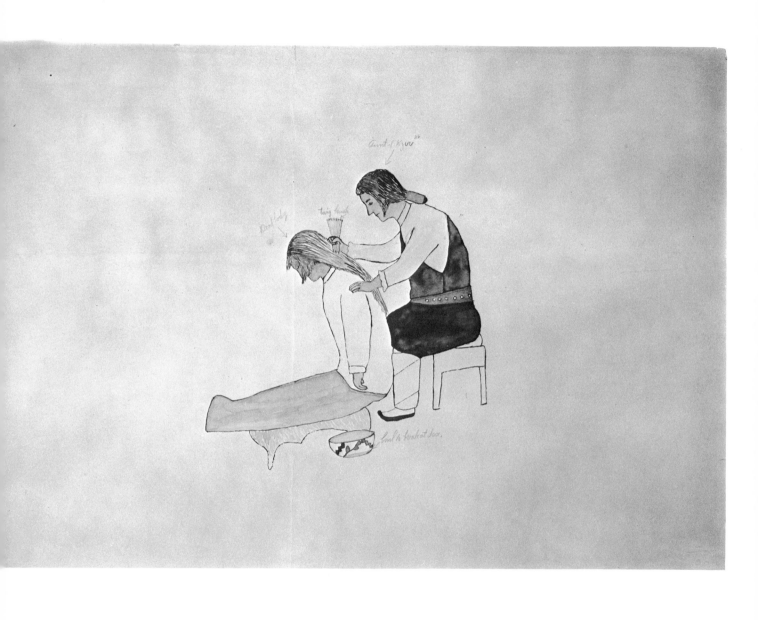

PAINTING 22

The White Corn Chief of Isleta died on December 17, 1940, and before any other preparation for burial was made, his successor, José Jojola, sang, and an assistant marked the body—cheeks, palms, knees, and insteps—with white, since the deceased belonged in "White Earth Way, east where the sun rises." José Jojola "is calling the deceased chief in song. At each call or mention of the deceased chief or of the east where the chief is placed [will go?], Patricio Luján, the assistant, marks the body," *just as meal is sprinkled to a spirit whenever he is referred to in song or prayer.*

The implication is that the deceased chief remains a chief in the East, in accordance with the general Pueblo belief that, after death, ceremonialists join their predecessors.

Powerful in life, the deceased White Corn Chief will also be powerful in death. That is why, I surmise, Felipe writes: "I don't want to mention his name. You can guess easy. Don't you write his name."

March 3, 1941

56

Pablo abeita death you see as he look died aloud mention his name in history Just say Indi Chief

When the the Chief or assistant died marking

No 2.

PAINTING 23

The corpse lies in the middle of the room, in a friarlike habit, mantas sewn together down the back, with three knots in the belt ends. The head rests on an adobe block. In the clasped hands is a cross. The candles at the feet are placed there by people who come to see the body.

All this is Spanish-Mexican custom, except that the shroud would represent, if anything, the array of San José.

May 18, 1937

58

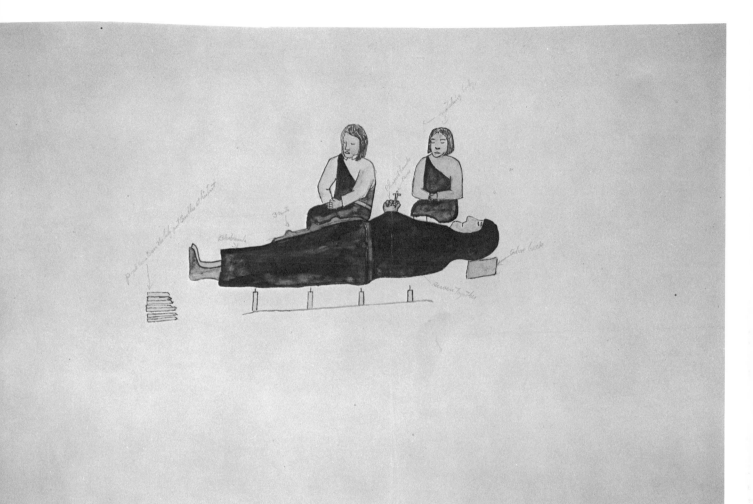

PAINTING 24

The funeral party makes a circuit around the churchyard. In each corner for a few minutes they rest the body. "They say this is the last time for him to go around where he used to walk in procession or at Mass when he was alive."

"Ramón Zuni is singing and praying, as Ramón is prayer [maker] and sings [chants] in Spanish for all ceremonials for the dead and for the saints. The people ask Ramón to pray when they need him. He is the last one left able to do this. If he dies there will be no one that can do all this. He is grandfather [Black Eyes], Laguna Father [medicine man], and prayer maker for all [Catholic] ceremonial. He looks exactly as in the drawing: dark complexion and bob hair, just as you see him, you can't mistake him."

Inferably, Father Dozier, who has been resident priest in Isleta for over 30 years, has not trained prayer makers or chanters, *rezadores* or *cantores*, in the Spanish Catholic way.

March 3, 1941

60

Parmor Juini

Rest here first Parmor.

prayers for anything removed.

4 Parmor,
last rest.

2 Parmor
Rest here

3 Parmor
rest here

Carry a dead around the place where he met to ascend in his life day   no 5
for the last

PAINTING 25

An actual funeral is being pictured, that of Remijo Lucero who died May 9, 1937, aged about 70. He succeeded Dolores Jojola as Chief of the War Society, Kumpawithlawen. Remijo was the oldest man in the society. For several years, until his death, he was acting Town Chief. Sun Arrow, the last "real" Town Chief died in the eighties. No successor was installed, so his "guard," the Bow Chief, Kabew'iride (Dolores Jojola), took his place.[16] When Dolores Jojola died, the Chief of the War Society (Kumpa), Remijo Lucero succeeded as acting Town Chief.

Like all ceremonialists at death, the face of the acting Town Chief is painted as in life when ceremonially engaged, and in his hair are two eagle feathers. The woman behind is carrying a jar of water to pour on the grave "so if the deceased gets thirsty he can have a drink."

[16] For a direct statement on these points by Felipe, see p. 4, note 4; cf. p. 8, note 7.—ESG.

May 18, 1937

62

The best service that I is place when *Pedro Gila died*
This man died just on may 9th 1937 the last oldest man.

Pomcas bueno

They always bury water to grow up poor ...
in case life finish as the —
deceased way if the city
to have a drink

This is the way they carry body to Church and to Grave.

PAINTING 26

The godmother stands at the child's head. Also present are the godfather, "aunt," little sister (or friend). A kinsman carries the cross.

"The godmother dresses a [deceased] child up to the age of 10. She makes a hat and decorates it with ribbons and flowers and puts flowers on the long skirts sewed together with ribbons of all colors. She paints the cheeks and chin red. This dressing means that the child died before sinning. He is without sin; they call him 'angel,' or 'little angel,' angelito."

All this is Spanish funerary custom for an *angelito*, a child dying before confirmation. The body is dressed as a saint (the face is not painted) and placed, as in the picture, on a table.

June 1940

64

God-mother

God father

God sister
or
Relative

Aunt

Taking out to
Dead

Relation
carrying Cross in front

no 5   Funeral for Acoh girl or boy or lady dress for burial

PAINTING 27

"Four men are holding the body in a blanket to hand it over to two others who are waiting in the hole. The other man is the watchman to see that the body is placed right, that feet and hands do not slip out and that the blanket is drawn off the face, all clear open to pour dirt." The body lies with head to the south. After it has been carefully placed, the two men standing in the grave are pulled up by their hands. Then they pray and begin to fill in the dirt.

A word about burial places. Offerings to the dead and to Weide are made on the four "ash piles" or middens, one on each side of town. From this fact, and from the taboos about these large refuse mounds and the dread they induce, it may be safely inferred that they are the early burial places or, at least, are so considered.

I put the question directly to Felipe. He answered, "Yes, long ago they used to bury the dead people in ash pile." He continued, "Then when Mexicans came first long ago, one or two Mexicans, they learned to bury people in one place. That was when they started the old campo santo. It was not fenced or in line, they just buried them. The very first man buried in this open campo santo was one of the richest old men. He had lots of sheep. His name was Ambrosio Lucero. Old woman María Abeita and an old man named Haka Biantue, mountain mark, were the others. These three persons were buried in the old graveyard over on the hill on the south side. Then they left that old campo santo and started to bury dead people in front of the churchyard. Not long ago they stopped burying the dead there because it was too crowded; they dug one up when they buried another. So Father Dozier told them to use the old campo santo which was in use before Dozier came."

Graveyard removals have always been resisted among the Pueblos and this latest removal at Isleta, if not the preceding ones also, caused "big trouble." The present cemetery lies southwest of town (south of Oraibi).

March 3, 1941

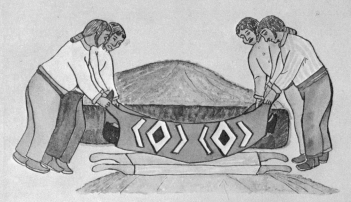

Barliing a dead in Grave

No.3

PAINTING 28

After the grave is half full, 3 feet of soil being thrown in, most of the people leave. Then the "aunt" who carries the water pours it into the grave "to give the dead person his last drink." All the "aunts" of the deceased do this in turn, each carrying water and each pouring it in. Then a male relative, but not father or brother, takes a mallet and pounds the soil, "striking the corpse first over the face, knocking the teeth out, then over all the body. They pound the dead to be sure that he is dead, and they pound hard and tighten the dirt. They claim if they do not pound, he (or she) may come to life and suffer in the dirt, so they give it to him (or her) extra heavy in order not to come to life in the grave. Sometimes after it is pounded the dirt lowers about 3 or 5 inches, then they say the dead one does not want to leave the world, he wants his family or relations to go with him."

"The mallet or block of wood is a knot of cottonwood weighing 50 pounds. It has two holes at the end so a man can put his fingers in tight, hold it up and strike as hard as he can. It was made a long, long time ago and we don't know who made it, it's so old. It is called boyua shoor la, dead-striker (pounder) wood. It is always left in the cemetery."

This drastic treatment is obviously exorcism of the deceased. Exorcism of ghosts is a general Pueblo practice but this particular form is unique—as far as I know. Indeed, it seems so extraordinary that were it not for the descriptive details the account would be incredible. The practice suggests that the dead at Isleta, at least the ordinary dead, are thought of, or were once thought of, as malevolent spirits. The role of deceased ceremonialists is not yet quite clear.

January 6, 1941

68

5

PAINTING 29

After burial the relatives stand together to be preached to. The relative in charge talks and prays: "Now our son [daughter] is called and taken. Our great father needs him more than we. Our great father needs him somewhere, maybe in Baptist religion [!] or in our poor Indian religion, so he took him away, and we give him to our Mother Earth to feed herself with the body. As one day or night he was born on this earth so one day or night he had to die. We miss the look of him, the shadow we miss. And we must return to his place where he made a poor living, where he lived poor, in order to discuss sending a man of his clan [Corn group] to eat and sleep at the dead person's house for 4 days, as is our poor Indian way if a person is willing to offer lovingly to do this."

Then they all pray and leave the grave and go straight to the house where the dead person used to live.

The spirit of the deceased lingers 5 days at his house, and we note from the above prayer that a member of his Corn group is expected to volunteer to stay with the household during this troublous, perhaps dangerous, period.

March 3, 1941

70

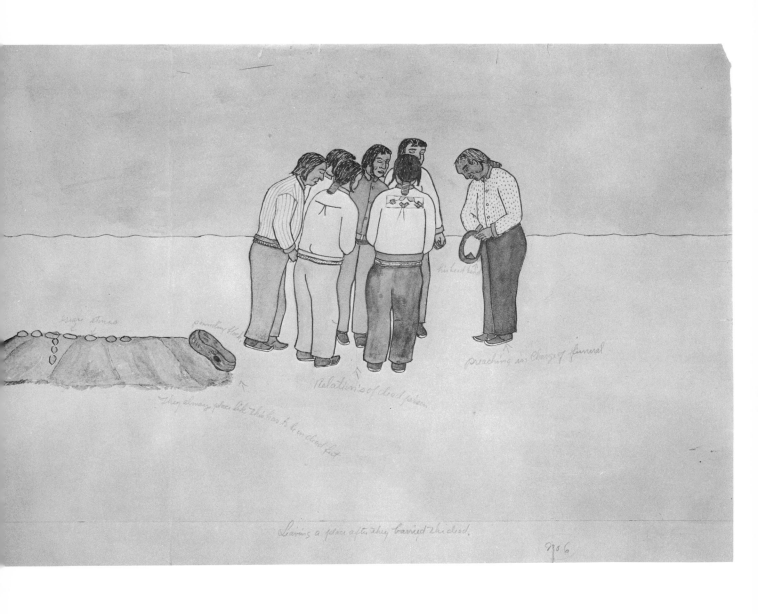

esque stones

something floss

his head bent

Relations of dead person

preaching in charge of funeral

They always place like this has to be in dead feet

Leaving a place after they buried the dead.

No 6

PAINTING 30

On the third day after the death, everybody who has stayed in the house has his or her head washed. On the fourth day, before sunrise, everybody goes to cast meal in the river and bathe. In the evening the Corn Fathers lay down their meal altar in the house of mourning and make a road of meal from the house door to the altar for the deceased. The Chief sprinkles all present from the medicine bowl on the altar. He sprinkles meal on the meal road, singing to the deceased to enter and eat. Then the Fathers take out the bowl of food and a bowl containing possessions of the deceased (his bow, arrows, and gourd rattle) and prayer feathers made for him by the Chief (cf. Painting 140). With duck feathers a Father sweeps away the road. They are going "to chase the deceased from the village."

Returning to the house, they will close the door, making a cross on it with a stone point. They will pass the stone point over the walls. They will tell all present "to forget it all; it is now 4 years he is dead."

Substituting years for days is characteristic of formal Pueblo speech. Making the sign of the cross in exorcism seems to be a Catholic rite. The Indian cross is a summons to the spirits, a road for them from all the directions.

February 15, 1937

72

Page 249

The father taking out the body of eat and his belonging Chase him out the deceased

PAINTING 31

Infants dying before baptism, also the stillborn, are not buried in the cemetery. They are taken out to Red Earth Hill *(Nampeikoto)*, to the southwest. "They don't dress the baby or give it anything, just take it out as it is. The Father [moiety chief] covers the infant with some dirt and rocks, but he does not bury it. Sometimes coyotes or dogs eat the body. The Father will turn the eumaune in all the directions that he (or she) may go back to the rain god(s) whence he came and, that when he arrives, it may rain. The Father prays to the directions and to the rain cloud god(s) so that it will rain when the eumaune reaches the rain god(s)."

"When the Father returns to the house he tells the mother not to think about the baby as he has already returned to the rain god(s). He may bring rain."

Here is a strong suggestion that formerly Isletans may have associated the dead in general with rainfall as do other Pueblos. We may also recall that the early Aztecs sacrificed children to the rain gods. In the Isletan tradition about Grandfather Stone (Parsons, 1932, p. 412) there is a hint of child sacrifice.

At the close of the winter solstice ceremonies of the Isletan Corn groups, prayer sticks, sacred meal, and food crumbs are deposited at Red Sand Hill for the infant rainmakers (ibid., pp. 299–300).

Before baptism Isleta infants may be referred to as "little Navaho" or "Coyote," a pseudonym for Navaho, because Navaho too are unbaptized. "My poor little Navaho," a mother will say. Among Andean Indians in Ecuador I found the term for the unbaptized or pagan Indians applied also to infants dying before baptism, and these infants, as at Isleta, are thought of as spirits, not angelitos or Catholic child spirits, but Indian spirits.

July 25, 1940

PAINTING 32

When a nursling dies "the mother will milk herself into a bowl, drop a piece of cotton in the milk, and throw the cotton onto the ceiling above the door, one piece every day for 12 days, to feed the baby. The baby is called little angel. They say the baby comes around to nurse. After 12 days, they say, the baby is gone forever."

In Pueblo opinion, infant spirits linger longer about their home than the spirits of deceased adults. In prehistoric times deceased infants were buried in the house, and Hopi believe they may be reborn to their mother.

Calling the baby little angel, angelito, is a general Spanish practice in accordance with the Catholic belief that before confirmation children are sinless and go directly to heaven.

"Twelve" is a favored Tiwa numeral, a stereotype for a long ritual period.

February 12, 1940

76

Cottonwood milk

Dotten on the ceiling upon from laws

Pole

Saint on wall

Bone for milk

No. 2D.

PAINTING 33

From December 1 to 20 the chiefs of the Corn groups, the Corn Fathers (often called Corn Mothers) hold their 4-day ceremonies separately but in no particular order, except that the White Corn Chief goes in a day ahead and the Shichu a day after the others. The ceremonies are for the Sun and it is known that at this time the Sun "turns south," but there is said to be no solar observation and apparently the ceremonies have no New Year character. (For a fuller account, see Parsons, 1932, pp. 290–301.)

All chiefs, who will function, visit the Salt Circle *(balimakore)* to get permission to hold their ceremony. "They don't get permission from Town chief or from any person. They ask permission from the Salt Circle, they ask for road. The Circle has been always there since the real old Town chief was alive. He left the Circle there when he died. The Circle is made with cornmeal of all colors because the Town chief is over every Corn group and over every ceremony." Only chiefs or members of the chiefly groups ever see this Circle. Townspeople in general know about the house of the Town Chief, but they don't know what is inside.

The Circle is crossed by lines pointing from east, west, north, south, and at the center is the triple fifth direction: up, down, and middle. "The lines are roads coming into the Circle and that is why they ask for a good road from all the directions."

"Under the Salt Circle in a pit are planted all kinds of animal meat and even birds of all kinds, mice, rats, deer, antelope, and so on. They claim that all our life is planted there, too, inside the Circle. The Town chief marked the Salt Circle and placed all kinds of lives inside."

Later information. In the pit in a buckskin bag (pit or bag is referred to as 'nest,' *ekue*) are "all kinds of animal life, also our life. That is why in prayer they always mention the middle of the Circle in Town chief's house where our life is."

"We are in one nest" is a Taos saying. I had taken it wholly metaphorically, but possibly at Taos, too, there is a ritual nest.

July 14, 1939

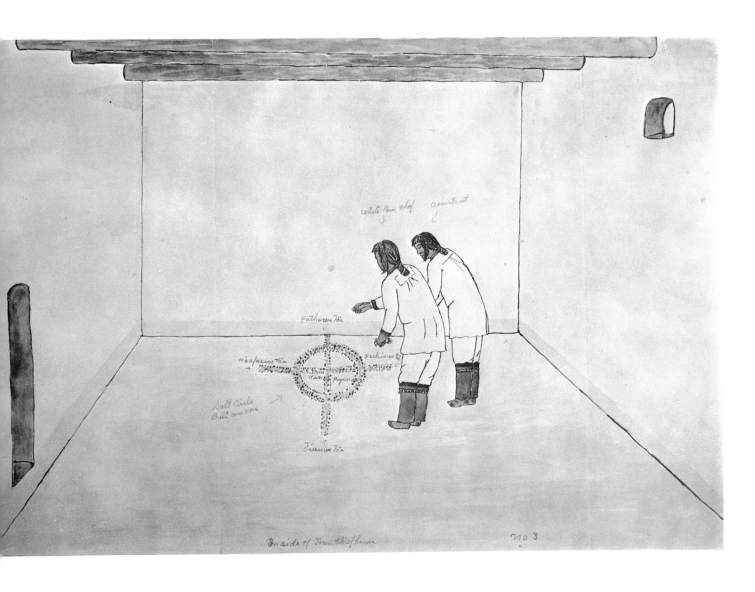

white Town chief   assistant

pâthw̓en Tôa

N̓oofaɛno Tôa →   pachimos Tôa

ǹ̓am pɛyem

Salt Circle
Buli'ma pona

Jiurnive Tôa

Inside of Town Chief house   No 3

PAINTING 34

During his winter solstice ceremony White Corn Chief, Chief of the Day People, comes out early every morning "to talk to the Sun." In his left hand he carries a basket of meal and *two duck feathers* and, in his right, some meal to cast to the Sun.

"He is asking the Sun for more power, asking to go strong on everything he does, asking health for himself and for all his people, and asking to have all the people feeling good toward him during his ceremony."

He will return to his ceremonial room "before people see him." On the last days of the ceremony the Chief is accompanied at dawn by his three assistants.

March 3, 1941

Tirwâr Sunkichatick

exactly as he was living

Poll Neih

Day people (white Corn Chief)   No 1

PAINTING 35

The third day of the retreat of the Corn Fathers, days of fasting and making prayer feathers, the Chief sends one of his "sons" for yucca or soapweed roots to make suds for hairwashing, always an important rite of purification among Pueblos.

Yucca, like many other plants or trees, is endowed with a spirit and must be approached with prayer and prayer meal. Plant or tree should be propitiated, and there should be no wasteful or wanton destruction. The plant or tree to be uprooted or cut is not asked for permission, but one nearby is—in this case, Yucca Old Woman.

As the "son" sprinkles meal from his meal pouch, he prays not to be punished for any "mistake," that is, offense to the plant.

July 14, 1939

82

Praying to old women ajarca getting permission To dig and get the root.
To take at Porn Chief house for head wash.

Porn Clan born in hill.   no 5.

PAINTING 36

On his return journey the messenger "thinks over what he is going to say to the Corn Father. He will tell him how he prayed to Yucca old woman, telling her his Corn name, and how he dug the yucca and carried it." Among Pueblos, ritual messengers are expected to relate every detail of their trip or journey.

The Corn Father will make a road of meal for the messenger from the door to the meal basket on the altar. The messenger will help himself to a pinch of meal which he will motion in the directions and cast toward the Sun. Then he will be given a cigarette and, after smoking it in the directions and toward the Sun, he will tell his story. The Father will thank him and give him permission to leave.

August 1, 1940

Ieppato corn white

yacca

he will tell his father corn chief what he pray to old man an yacca and told his corn name who cling her and raising her

Coming with bundle of yacca to Corn Chief Ceremony house. thinking what to tell chief and pray to [...]

PAINTING 37

Women are associated with all the ceremonial groups and the women members are regularly referred to as "mothers." They perform duties usual to women: supplying food, cleaning up, washing hair, fetching clay and water. They have few strictly ritualistic functions. But in fetching water for their Chief (early in the morning "before people will see them") they cast prayer sticks or prayer feathers made by the Chief and prayer meal into the river for the Water People.

March 18, 1938

Pl. 36

PAINTING 38

Before sunrise on the fourth day of the ceremony of the Corn groups, the chiefs go in line to the river to wash their hands and face and pray, "facing east, facing the sunrise." They will breathe on their prayer meal, motion it in the directions, and cast it into the river for the Water People. They will also cast meal to the Sun, asking him to let them remain alive while he journeys southward. As noted before, Sun Father is the source of life and longevity.

Breathing on or from sacred objects is an important rite among Pueblos.

June 20, 1939

88

At River early in morning before sun Rise

No.1

assistant

yellow Sun chief

Coming to River

praying at River facing out to sun Rise

white sun Chief

assistant

PAINTING 39

The women members of every ceremonial group wash the hair of the male members or chiefs.

Hair washing quite generally precedes ceremonial, and sometimes concludes it, among Pueblos. Note yucca roots on the floor for making suds.

April 6, 1937

90

Page 286 hair washing for medicine man or rain society

PAINTING 40

After the hair of the Fathers has been washed, toward noon, the time when the Sun stands still each day, the Chief dances, "showing him the prayer feathers he is to come and get." The Chief's helpers sing, "to call the Sun," which will stream through the roof hole.

The Sun journeys daily across the sky, it is believed, coming out from his house in the east and, after the noonday pause, going down to his house in the west.

92

Roof hole window   After hair washed. At noon Dancing to sun

the Chief Dancing showing prayfeathers to some can get it

suning for the sun fall

PAINTING 41

A "mother" has given the Chief a basket of meal of the color of their Corn group. The Chief lays his prayer feathers on the meal and then sprinkles them with meal. All this to song (see Parsons, 1932, p. 292).

Obviously a sun ray is being refracted by crystal, Hopi style. There was no doubt in the mind of my early informant that the Sun really did come down, get his feathers, and go up again, through the roof hole.

Knowing the "work" that is being done in the ceremonial rooms, the townspeople at this time remain in their houses and say a prayer to the Sun.

Undated

Roof hole

Aiming for the sun telling the sun to get his feathers

Chief place

Chief

Holding Sun to tie prayfeathers

history on page 292

PAINTING 42

Bits from all these bowls will be offered at the ash piles to Weide and the dead, dropped from the right hand for Weide, from the left for the dead. The Chief will put a piece in the mouth of each helper and in turn will be given a piece to eat (reminiscent of the Mass?). He then gives all present permission to eat. It is a ritual meal. Leftovers are distributed and carried home. A portion is carried to the Town Chief.

Throughout the Pueblos, the left side—left hand, left foot—is associated with the dead.

March 18, 1938

96

Food Distribution Figure 12.

PAINTING 43

The Black Eyes also hold a ceremony at the early winter ceremonial season, about December 10 or 13, "since they are winter people," and the four chiefs must have their hair washed.

When these moiety chiefs came out into the world at the Emergence, the Black Eyes from *Shipapu* Spring, they had no "mothers" or women helpers, so now the little girls who serve them in fetching water and washing hair are called "little old women" as surrogates for "mothers" such as are in attendance on the other groups. In view of the early warlike associations of the moiety chiefs, I surmise that girls who had not yet menstruated were considered the only proper or safe female helpers. There are taboos against menstruants in connection with hunting and warring among Tiwa as well as Hopi.

One "Little Old Woman" is washing the Chief's hair. The other stands ready with her gourd to rinse it.

After the washing the Chief will go through the door, as indicated, into the room where his helpers are waiting, and he will send out each in turn. In this room they keep the fetishes (*wahtainin*, 'life people').

August 31, 1939

98

PAINTING 44

The Red Eyes hold their ceremony in June, "since they are summer people."
Each moiety has its own "little old women."

August 13, 1939

Lu'li'gun oldmen

N4.

PAINTING 45

The Black Eye moiety chiefs, the *Shifunkaben,* are fasting in their ceremonial house. They are giving medicine water to the women. "The Black Eye chief is sitting by the fireplace holding duck feathers. One helper is giving a woman medicine water. Another is dipping medicine water into a bowl for the woman to take home and sprinkle in her rooms. Another woman is praying at the kitu, the village [as the altar meal design is called]. Another woman with her little girl is awaiting her turn. The little old women are sitting against the wall, they have been fasting too."

The child has been brought in "in order that she may know where she belongs. This is the way they begin to teach their children. This way the children know when they grow up where they belong."

"From this Black Eye medicine you may have good luck and good health. It will protect you from anything bad and give you good thoughts to find good luck [a blessing]." After the drink, the helper says

awashie	*uköweje*
you life (stone) knife	may (you) be old

Among Pueblos a sip of medicine water is the blessing always given members of his group by a chief.

The marks on the hands and feet of the chiefs are dark blue *(kofanta)*. They are the only chiefs who use this blue. It comes from a mesa where the source of the pigment is known only to the chiefs, and "they don't tell." Kofanta is used on Black Eye prayer sticks (Painting 140), and at the opening of the irrigation ditch it is offered to the Sun by the Black Eyes by flipping from the fingers.

October 13, 1939

PAINTING 46

A sick woman may promise to wash the Child of the Virgin *(niuude)*. The day before Christmas in the morning the "Mother Virgin" and the Child are carried to the house of the convalescent. The Virgin is placed on an improvised altar and the Child is bathed in "some kind of oil." A "watchman" stands on guard all day, and throughout the day the church bell is rung.

Vows *(promesa)* by the sick (or by their parents) are often made by the Pueblos of the Rio Grande, as in Mexico. It has been open to question in some cases whether the practice was aboriginal or Spanish. In Isleta it is plainly of Catholic origin.

Note the "little shirt for the baby so he will be born clean."

January 6, 1941

washing the little war-oʻula

had dust for baby as he is to be clean

At funeral house

PAINTING 47

Christmas Eve the convalescent and other women carry Virgin and Child back to the church to a place "made clean for them." During the little procession the watchman has fired his gun "every 5 minutes, every little while." As soon as the images are replaced in church the bell ceases to ring; then the dancers and choir arrive.

January 6, 1941

106

PAINTING 48

Before the midnight Mass there is dancing in the church by moiety, the two groups alternating, a dance pattern very familiar in the Rio Grande Pueblos. Black Eye men wear a sparrow-hawk feather headdress, Red Eye men, a headdress of turkey feathers. (These are the feathers regularly associated with the respective moieties.) Black Eye women dancers carry turkey feathers; Red Eye women, eagle feathers. (Felipe is depicting a Red Eye group, although he includes one sparrow-hawk headdress, why, I don't know.)

Church dancing was early Spanish usage, probably introduced by the friars, in Indian terms, "to please the Saint," and then fitted by the Indians into their own organization for dancing.

January 23, 1939

108

SANTA MARIA DANCE

n0 4

PAINTING 49

The Child, *El Niño*, as drawn, looks curiously like a stone fetish. The five-pointed star is probably European, although five is a favored Tiwa numeral. Three and, as noted, twelve are also favored.

January 20, 1938

110

Christmas eve. in church.

nopöashoti Nightdance

PAINTING 50

After the dance and the midnight Mass the birth of the Child is dramatized. "A woman sits in front of the altar, the baby in her lap just as the baby Christ was born." (At Zuni, dramatization of the birth has a more aboriginal aspect. The male kachina personator of *Chakwena* Woman lies in 4 days, and women who would conceive visit her to make gifts or dress her hair.)

Again vows are fulfilled. Any woman who in childbirth "has promised the Infant a shirt if she comes out all right" will present it at this time.

People kneel before the Child, pray, and "smell the baby," an interesting paraphrase for the breath rite. Among the Pueblos all sacred things are breathed from. Here we have a merging of the Catholic rite of kissing and the Indian rite of inhalation, the product being called smelling!

January 6, 1941

112

At Church Christmas Night

No. 5

PAINTING 51

One of the Christmas dances that may be performed outdoors during the 4 days of dancing after Christmas.

June 1940

PAINTING 52

The Christmas celebration of the Laguna colony at Oraibi is on Kings' Day, January 6, Old Christmas. From the Governor of Isleta the Town Chief of Keresan Oraibi will get permission to present the dance in Isleta itself. Then he calls on the Town Chief and the moiety chiefs. Before the Laguna colonists dance, Isleta people must dance by moiety. Only a few Isletans know the Laguna dance and are invited to dance with the Oraibi colonists. The dance is not familiar *because it is a ceremonial dance.* This picture shows why it is so considered, something I failed to appreciate fully before I saw it.

The Oraibi Town Chief (who is also Kachina Chief) is casting meal toward the dance tablets as if they were masks. Inferably the back tablets are, like masks, sacrosanct. "Without permission the dancer's back would blister and he would get sick. This has often happened."

Hopi use Sun tablets, one of many parallels between Hopi and western Keres indicating a sometime close relationship.

June 20, 1939

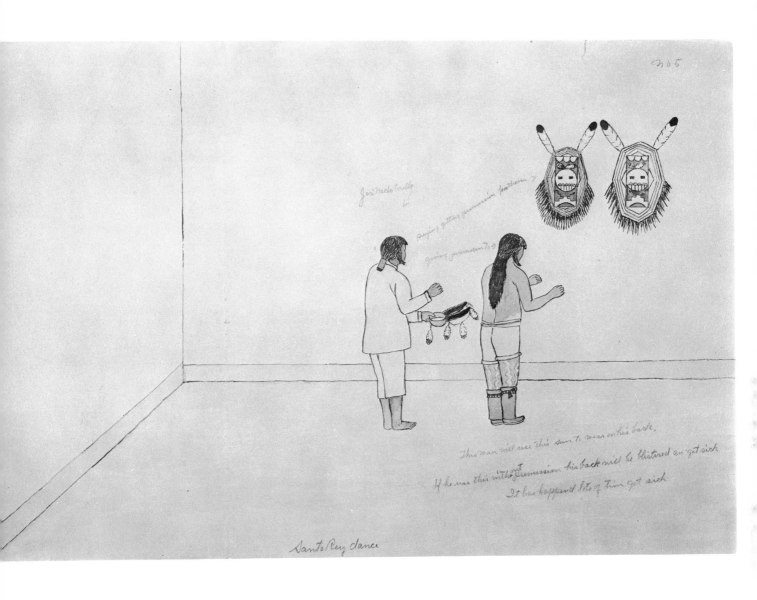

José Nacho Crillo

praying getting permission feathers ⟶

giving permission to ⟶

This man will use this sun to wear on his back.

If he use this with out permission his back will be blistered an get sick

It has happened lots of time get sick

Santo Rey dance

PAINTING 53

Kings' Day Dance continues for 4 days, more dancers taking part each day, beginning with eight dancers in each of the two alternating sets.

The first performance is inside the church, the night of January 5, in Spanish terms, *las visperas*, 'the Vespers Dance.' The next day the dancers perform in front of the houses of the newly elected town officers, in Rio Grande style, as well as in the churchyard.

November 1936

118

Page 306   Laguna King Dance on January

P A I N T I N G 5 4

The evening of the day they conclude the Kings' Day Dance by the Laguna colony, January 10, the Town Chief summons all the chiefs and the war captains to his ceremonial house to tell them they are going to look after the crops, and if they see anything bad about to come to take it away. He says he has chosen the chiefs of the medicine societies to help him, and he bids them go to their ceremonial houses and wait there for the war chief [Cane Chief, almost surely] and war captain.

The Town Chief appoints two couples, each consisting of a war chief [Cane Chief or his opposite in the Red Eye moiety, almost surely] and a war captain, a couple to go to each of the two medicine society chiefs to request the Fathers to hold the *Shunad,* the ceremony of general cleansing for the people, village, and fields.

January 30, 1938

message from Town chief

PAINTING 55

Among Pueblos, orders, generally in connection with a ceremony, are called out from rooftop or street, in this case from one of the ash piles or mounds, by a war captain. The Governor or one of his officers will call out orders for secular matters.

To build fires outside during a ceremonial period is a taboo also among other Pueblos. It has been interpreted sometimes as a blackout against enemy attack at a time when men are off guard. I was told that the Isletan war captain also calls out not to dig the ground or go out to work, taboos observed at Taos too, but, earlier, during the period of "staying still" in the winter ceremonies corresponding to those of the Isletan Corn groups and moiety societies.

March 18, 1939

122

The war Chief Calling out that they are going to have shuri'ed. not to build fire outside.

PAINTING 56

Following his first call the war chief [see p. 120] announces a rabbit hunt for the Fathers.

Rabbit drives are made customarily by all Pueblos in connection with ceremonies, Catholic and non-Catholic. In the Eastern Pueblos the hunt is managed by the war captains or Clown societies, and the meat is eaten by the ceremonialists or dancers and offered to the spirits.

Here, and manifestly after the hunt, one war captain is sprinkling salt on the rabbits lying on sheepskin, while another is cooking rabbits in the oven.

April 14, 1938

PAINTING 57

The War Chief is in the lead, making the road. The Fathers will eat these ritual food offerings *(laide)* after their fast of 4 days, during which time they touch neither food nor water. Among other Pueblos, fasting is not as rigorous, usually one meal being permitted and abstention extending only to meat and salt, or greasy or sweet foods.

March 14, 1938

126

These supplies are taken to the house of medicine societies

PAINTING 58

The fourth day of the ceremony of purification is public and all the townspeople will visit the house of one or the other medicine society, Town Fathers or Laguna Fathers.

The Chief of the Laguna Medicine Society is marked in white with the design of a bear paw; male members, the helpers, with lightning design. Women members wear a Hopi ceremonial mantle and, like the men, three eagle feathers in the hair. The Isleta Medicine Society, the Town Fathers, have no body painting. The face painting of both societies is the same, a red line and a black line across the nose and red and black parallels from each corner of the mouth horizontally across the cheeks.

The animal figurines *(kechu)* are of the animals from whom the Fathers get their power to cure or fly or combat witches: Bear, Eagle, Mountain Lion, Badger. They are transferred from the "medicine basket," near the Chief's right foot "into the water a mother is bringing," before the bowl is placed on the altar.

March 11, 1937

128

making medicine water before placing in altar

putting keechu in water.

PAINTING 59

With their feathers the Fathers "clean" the chamber and the people, exorcising witchcraft. At the doorway they will cleave feather against feather for Wind to carry away the evil.

Among Pueblos, ceremonies, particularly public ceremonies, are believed to be occasions of danger, attracting not only the spirits, but witches.

April 14, 1938

130

Town fathers

Truhi, truhi!
Truhi, truhi!

Truhi, truhi!
Truhi, truhi!

Cleaning the road and the people with feathers

Page 313

PAINTING 60

One Father is sucking a witch-sent "rag from a woman's body"; another is pulling from his mouth the "rag" he has sucked out. He will deposit it in the bowl near his feet. As he carries out the bowl the people will spit toward it. (Spitting is often a rite of exorcism among Pueblos. Is it aboriginal? If so, it curiously parallels the European folkway of spitting in disgust or contempt.)

[For the record I include here excerpts from Dr. Parsons' commentaries attached to paintings dealing with the public part of the Shunad, the Cleansing ceremony. These paintings, which apparently depict the activities of the Laguna Fathers, were among those not available at the time of printing.—ESG.]

On the final night of the Cleansing ceremony, a series of rituals is performed publicly. "Clay Old Woman" has been fetched by the women, for clay forms the base of the "Corn Mothers," perfectly kerneled ears of white corn, wrapped with cotton and dressed with beads and feathers.

Before the Fathers go out "to clean the village," they dance and impersonate animals. The Chief and one helper remain behind and sing. Crop-destroying creatures, placed in the field by witches, are captured and burned later; sometimes also a witch doll. (Kumpa "closes the road" to witches by drawing a line.)

In the ceremonial room Medicine Society Chief pulls down a rabbit and by marking a circle around it with his stone point "ties it so it cannot move away." He also produces a cornstalk with ripened ears. He gives three seeds from the Corn Mothers, or magically from corn murals, to the officiants and spectators—and a sip of water. As he offers the latter, he prays: "With this medicine water (*lifiewah*) you are fed. May you have good luck and live to old age." One Father then waves the Corn Mothers to the people "to take breath from them," while two others take the stone points from the altar and place them in a deerskin bag, leaving it in a corner of the ceremonial room. Then the people go home.

Later in the day the Fathers take out the prayer sticks made during their retreat for the fields and address them to the Sun and to weather.

June 15, 1936

132

PAINTING 61

The Fathers have the power of flight, power from Eagle. They use this power to fetch spruce for their dance or, if requested, for any dance. "In a quarter of an hour they reach the mountain and are back again." They wear ritualistic moccasins of painted buckskin *(sumkup)* similar to those of the Town Chief.

March 11, 1937

134

Brushshin moccasins.

quarter of a hare being stands from mountain. They fly in pieces. They wear Sunokey.

PAINTING 62

The walls of the Town Fathers' house are undecorated. The eagle-wing feathers stuck into the pillar and the bear paws hanging on the wall (when they are not needed in a ceremony) were "used by old medicine men, dead long ago. Real corn and wheat from the fields are kept on the wall. The water jar is always kept filled. In an old box in the wall they keep the Sun that is made with little sticks and feathers. After the night ceremonial [for crops and well-being], around 4 o'clock in the morning, the medicine chief opens the box and holds the Sun in his hand as it opens all around; people dance with the chief. Then they give people permission to go home."

The ritual object referred to as "Sun" is described as if it were a fan. I have never succeeded in getting a better description of it. (See Parsons, 1932, p. 446, for the Town Father who flies.)

June 1940

136

PAINTING 63

Note the mural paintings of the curer animals—Mountain Lion [looking very much like an African lion], Bear, Badger, Rattlesnake, and Eagle—of Sun, Moon, and Star, Corn, and the kachina. There are two striking variations in Felipe's mural from that of the Laguna Fathers given in Parsons, 1932, plate 17. In the latter, the anthropomorphic spirits are without masks and the star is five-pointed. In Felipe's mural the star is four-pointed and the human figures are masked. Both artists are Isletans, but Felipe has some Laguna associations. The draftsman of plate 17 was undoubtedly drawing according to stereotype, by preconception—a good illustration of *Gestalt psychologie* [cf. also frontispiece, present publication, which is dated September 9, 1940].

June 1940

138

no 3.

PAINTING 64

This is a rain ceremony of the Laguna Fathers held at night in February just before planting.

The Laguna Fathers have laid out their altar and are dancing before it—*natoypör* (Prayer Stick Dance?). The women and boy hold prayer sticks made by the Fathers. These sticks are given to persons present at the ceremony to place in their fields before planting.

Keresan societies have weather as well as curing or cleansing ceremonies.

January 6, 1938

140

PAINTING 65

The day following their night ceremony the Laguna Fathers dance outdoors, in "laplaza." The women carry an ear of corn in each hand and, I infer from dance gestures among Keres, they raise first one arm and then the other. The men carry gourd, rattle, and lightning stick, as this is a dance for rain. Note bells under the left knee, and a turtle-shell rattle under the right knee—the leg rattles of all the Pueblos—and the kachina dance kilt and belt. Presumably the Fathers are impersonating the kachina.

April 6, 1939

This is Laguna futuro dance in February that picture I sent you to get their spound they dance now to day

PAINTING 66

Thliwa (maskless kachina) dances take place in February, March, and September. At the February dance (*Thliwapör*, also called Turtle Dance) which is performed by moiety by two alternating sets both outdoors and in the Round House (Fog or Mist Kiva) at night, it is the duty of the Chief of the Yellow Corn group, sometimes referred to as Earth or Yellow Earth Chief, to build the fire at the night dance. Fire is associated with his group.

Yellow Earth Chief is the only man allowed to build the fire at the Round House whenever there is a ceremony. War Chief (Kumpa) with a cigarette asks the Earth Chief to build a fire, and Earth Chief carries his slow match *(wikun)* to Town chief's house where a fire is made with flint and cotton.

Earth Chief lights the fire in front of the fire screen, with cloud design, and facing the south arc of the kiva where the ladder descends, he sings "about how he is getting fire from the east, north, west, south, and middle." He puts the slow match to the wood when in song "he calls the middle." He does this before people come in. "I know all these songs," writes Felipe. "I wish I could sing for you. It's big interesting."

No one who comes into the kiva for dance or ceremony is permitted to use American matches. A cigarette wrapped in cornhusk is the only smoke allowed, and no one may get a light for himself. The Earth Chief's helper has to stand by all the time with his fire stick to give smokers a light. After lighting his cigarette, the smoker returns the stick, thanking the Fire Chief [Earth Chief's helper] and saying, *"Tauu kaan keminen hawashe ini kimhecha,"* 'may the great Father or Mother take care of you!'

The ritual cigarette is referred to as *pakimu*, fog or mist, as at Zuni. The War Chief of Isleta uses other special words or expressions (Parsons, 1932, p. 258). War language or chiefly language is a widespread Indian trait.

March 29, 1939

144

(Hé Kamis)

Ladder

in 7 to all the round et

Bessae

Cloud design   fire throw

fire serum t   earth chief given over

Inside round Kva south end

PAINTING 67

When the dancers are ready to go to the Round House, Black Eye Moiety Chief gives the Black Eye grandfathers permission to go first. When they arrive at the Round House they knock with their yucca blades at the ladder entrance. "Then the people inside all get scared. They sit close so there will be plenty of room for the dancers." War Chief (Kumpa), who is present in the middle of the floor, answers the grandfathers, "*Akuamhura machead,*" 'greetings same to you, come in!' (As the dancers step on the ladder to come in, one after another rattling his gourd, War Chief answers in the same way: "*Akuam machede him kaa waean,*" 'greetings, come in, my Fathers.')

When the grandfathers first come in, before the dance, they go around and clean—posts, ladder, fireplace, and fire screen in the middle—just as the medicine men do with their eagle feathers, but the grandfathers clean with yucca blades. Elsewhere in the Kachina cult yucca whips are used in exorcism on house walls and persons. At Isleta ritual flagellation for breaking taboos appears not to be practiced. [In view of the use of the dreaded punishment circle (cf. Painting 103) and the functioning of the kapyo as ceremonial police (cf. Painting 85), as well as the fact that this commentary itself mentions the fright of the people when the Black Eye grandfathers clear the way with their yucca whips, it is difficult to believe that, whatever the situation when these pictures were submitted, flagellation was not practiced at Isleta at an earlier time. Quite possibly, nearness to the United Pueblos Agency at Albuquerque, which can serve conveniently as a court of appeals, was enough to eliminate a very general mode of Pueblo discipline.]

Back of the fire screen in a pit is the blue cornbread and tortilla always placed there for the *teliefpoyan,* the Navaho dead. "They always have to have their food so they don't get hungry and make a noise." Among Tanoans, scalps are supposed to be able to whistle or cry and of themselves to drop from their wall niche. Scalps give warning of enemy approach. They are not rainmakers as at Zuni.

March 29, 1939

Dakimna or Kleyu

The two chiefs smoking kiastihn
and popoimo tube to the person

north side of Kiva

no. 3

PAINTING 68

At the head of the dancers stand the Black Eye Chief and *Chakabede,* who is both Thliwa Chief and the Chief of Yellow Corn or Yellow Earth People. At the other end of the dance line stand a grandfather, a war captain, and a medicine man who guard the road against bad people (witches) lest they hurt the kachina. Yellow Earth Fire Man stands ready to give a light to smokers. In front of him sit three men of the Yellow Earth or Yellow Corn hierarchy. War Chief (Kumpa) sits on a red blanket on the other side of the fire screen (in line with Fire Chief). Note, behind fire screen, the pit for "the Navaho dead" and in front of fire screen, beyond the fire, the pit in which are kept the wahtainin, all the stone fetishes.

This picture has considerable significance in relation to the ceremonial organization of Isleta. All the distinctive ceremonial groups are represented: moiety, through Black Eye Chief and Black Eye grandfathers; Corn group, through Yellow Corn or Yellow Earth functionaries in control of part of the Thliwa cult and fire; medicine society, through a watchful medicine man; and the permanent War Society, through its Chief. The secular government is also represented by the annual war captain, among the Pueblos ever a partly ceremonial and partly secular official.

Obviously the grandfathers fill the role of the sacred clowns (masked and unmasked at Zuni, unmasked elsewhere, possessed of masks at Taos), who generally accompany the kachina.

There are two sets of dancers, Black Eyes and Red Eyes, who alternate in the kiva and in the plaza where they dance 2 to 4 days.

February 29, 1939

148

PAINTING 69

Shichu is the All Colors Corn group that "goes in" last at the solstice ceremonies. The group is associated with the Town Chief in racing, representing the Moon, and in opening irrigation; in myth it is associated with Bat, from whom the Chief gets his power. The night of the Thliwa dance this group also presented a dance which preceded the Thliwa dancing, but in recent years this Shichu Dance has lapsed. The Shichu Chief appointed the dancers from his group, from his "children," and they practiced in his house.

Before the dance Shichu Chief held a ceremony to make prayer feathers, to receive infants into the group, give them their Corn name, and offer members a drink of his medicine water.

March 11, 1937

150

Shichu Dance   on page 318

PAINTING 70

There is another kachina dance in February or March, Dark Kachina, for the crops, and on the second day of the dance there is a rabbit drive. The temporary moiety clowns, the kapyo, have fetched spruce for the dancers the day before the dance commences and erected a spruce tree in the plaza (cf. Paintings 109, 111). The head kapyo climbs the tree and calls out that "people must get ready their hunt lunch, that they will go out east, north, west, south, to catch rabbits, little and big. All the clowns go up in turn and each will call down, 'My Fathers, what shall I shake down for you?' They all laugh and tease the one on top. They might tell him, if he is Shiu clan (Eagle Corn Group), 'Throw down some mice from your pocketful!' They all laugh, also the people. They always ask for something funny so they will laugh."

Was this tree climb the prototype of the pole climb of Taos?

February 13, 1939

152

PAINTING 71

The dancers go hunting for the grandfathers. In the evening they return to the kiva singing, the grandfathers in the lead loaded with rabbits, the three Thliwa chiefs (Chakaben) and dancers following them. The rabbits are placed on the floor of the kiva, their heads to the east. "They feed the rabbits by sprinkling meal on them."

In this way among Pueblos game animals are always "fed." It is a prayer to their departing spirits to send their children in future hunts—as naive a manifestation of the egoism of man as our own belief that God created the animals for man's use.

February 13, 1939

154

Grand Fathers

Chakaden

Dancers

PAINTING 72

While the Dark Kachina Dance is going on in the Round House, the grand-fathers will take the rabbits that were caught the previous day to the plaza "where the women chase after them." This chasing of clowns for what they are carrying has been called "wrangling" among the Hopi. It is not a practice at Taos. Possibly Isletans picked it up during their sojourn among the Hopi, just as did the Jemez visitors to Hopiland.

April 6, 1937

156

Page 264 Shush Grand fathers

PAINTING 7 3

The woman who captures a rabbit from a grandfather is expected to pay him with food. The grandfather in the lead is carrying a bowl of stew and the woman carries a bowl of bread. The other grandfather is carrying her rabbit for her.

Among other Pueblos when women go on the rabbit drive, the woman first to reach the hunter is given the rabbit and the next day she in turn gives the hunter a bowl or basket of food. This practice does not occur among Tiwa, but at Isleta women may be given rabbits at the conclusion of the hunt (cf. Painting 121) and again, as we see, they may wrangle them from the grandfathers.

June 15, 1936

Grandfathers earning his return pay after this woman get the rabbit

Figure 4 Lee

PAINTING 7 4

The masked Kachina cult flourishes among the Laguna colonists in the Isleta suburb of Oraibi. The Oraibi Town Chief serves as Kachina Chief, but as there is no kiva at Oraibi, night ceremonies are held in the house of the Laguna Fathers in Isleta proper.

The Oraibi Kachina Chief whirls his rhombus in front of his altar before "he starts his kachina to dance." Chakwena and *Kumeoishi* masks are on the altar, also medicine bowl.

Kumeoishi *(koyemshi)* is the clown mask of the western Pueblos. Chakwena is a familiar kachina, but elsewhere the mask is black. Note also water jar for sprinkling, and medicine man, a Laguna Father, sitting and guarding against witches.

The rhombus is used in weather ritual among the western Pueblos, and sometimes, it is said, against witches.

May 18, 1937

160

page 354

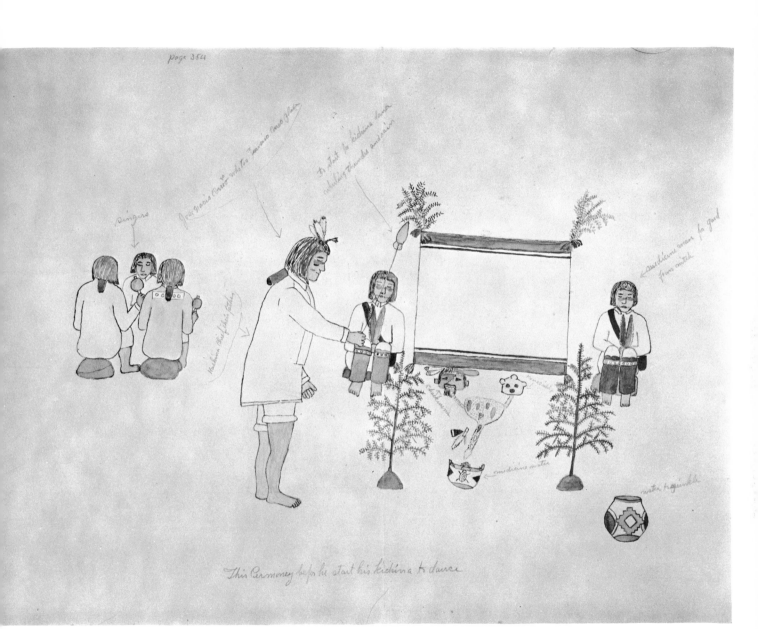

This Ceremony befor he start his Kichina to dance

PAINTING 75

This kachina dance is being performed in the Laguna Father's house. The Oraibi Kachina Chief stands in front. The kachina facing him is like Aiyayaode, opines Felipe, adding that in Oraibi he is referred to as Kachina Hunt Chief. The kachina in the center is said by Isletans to be their *Thliwa Funide,* Dark Kachina. The third kachina calls Oho! Oho! "He is mean; he used to kill children." (In Laguna terms these three are Duck, *Nawish* and *Hilili*—not *chapio,* as Felipe believed). Juan Rey Sheride (or Churina), "a powerful medicine man," stands at the end, with eagle feathers and stone point; to the left are two singers and the drummer. The drum is a pottery bowl, "different from all other drums."

This dance may also be given outdoors in Isleta, sometime between Shunad and the summer solstice ceremonies. With these masked dancers under their eyes and with two of them equated with their own kachina spirits, it is remarkable that Isletans have not taken to using kachina masks, a very interesting instance of failure to borrow.

March 10, 1939

162

Francisco Padilla 2005

Jose Nacio Real/b Kachina Chief

Láte Oi gayaho

Falting o hoi oboi
hi is many

Juan Rey Acheurda,
grassfal medicine

Night Kachina Ceremony at Laguna fathers house

No 4

PAINTING 76

Before irrigation ceremonial and work on the ditch there is a ritual against grasshopper invasion, ever a threat to the crops.

Among Pueblos, grasshopper plagues are commonly thought to be caused by witches, generally witches in another town. They "plant" a grasshopper, inferably from our pictures, the Grasshopper Chief whom his people will follow. The Isletan Town Father is anticipating the witches by capturing Grasshopper Chief in advance. Medicine men and witches have similar power, only their ends differ.

War Chief (Kumpa) and war captain will wait on this hill, about 2 or 3 miles from town, for the Medicine Society Chief to return from his mission. War Chief, his insignia alongside, is smoking in the directions, asking for power.

April 18, 1939

164

going after Grasshopper Chief.

Kuampa waiting out on hill when melons Chief gone

PAINTING 77

The Town Father is carrying Grasshopper Chief in a bowl. The others are guarding against witches who are abroad, attempting to get possession of Grasshopper Chief.

Witchcraft is a momentous and horrendous problem to all Pueblos, a danger which not only their medicine men but their War chiefs must face and control. Witches are always lurking about while rituals or dances are being performed, so that War chiefs or war captains are constantly in attendance as guards.

March 18, 1939

166

noq   73

PAINTING 78

This picture is particularly significant for the study of the ceremonial organization of Isleta. The Town Fathers are represented and the chiefs of all the Corn groups. The War Chief and war captains are not shown, but as their insignia (the War Chief's bow and arrows and bandoleer and the canes of the war captains) are on the altar, they are undoubtedly in attendance, a war captain probably on guard outside.

The Corn Fathers (also called Mothers) or Chiefs of all the Directions are the Chiefs of the Day People or White Corn (east), Magpies (or Shrikes) and Poplars or Black Corn (north), Earth People or Yellow Corn (west), Water-Bubble and Cane-Blowing People or Blue Corn (south), Corn People or Corn of all Colors (up, down, and middle), Eagle People and Goose People or Corn of all Colors (up, down, and middle), Shichu or Corn of All Colors (up, down, and middle).

The Town Fathers sit singing behind the altar near which rests the bowl containing Grasshopper Chief covered over. Women members of the Medicine Society are seated along the wall. The seven Corn chiefs, the Chiefs of all the Directions, stand praying and taking breath from the corn fetishes on the altar.

April 18, 1939

168

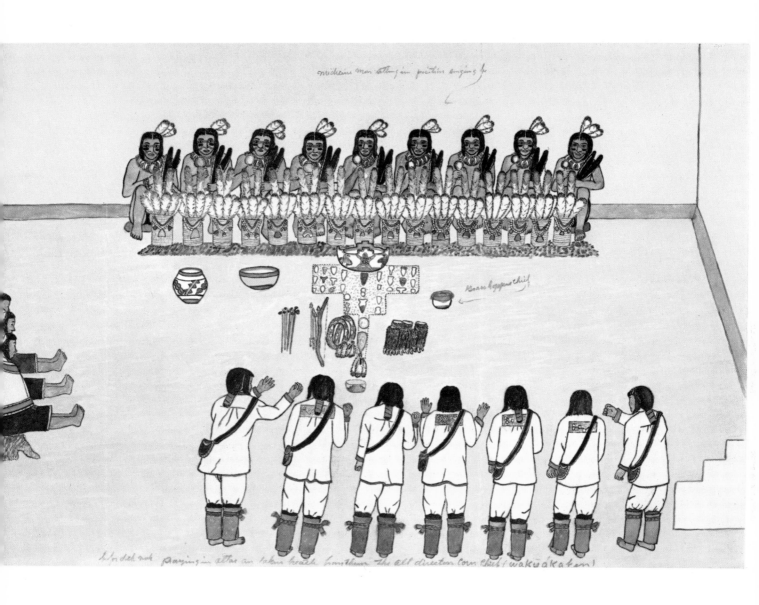

medicine man sitting in position singing by

bear leggens chief

before deh nah praying in altar an taken heads from them the alt direction corn chief (wakisakaken)

PAINTING 79

Town Chief, War Chief (Kumpa), Shichu Chief, and War Chief of the Cane are setting out from Town Chief's house to give a prayer stick to Weide and request that the people be permitted to start work on the irrigation ditches.

Irrigation is an important part of Pueblo agriculture, whether by flood or ditch, and before planting, townsmen clean and repair ditches as a communal service. In connection with work on the ditch, ritual is always performed, generally in relation to water spirits who control the flow. Felipe implies that "cutting the earth," digging, also requires ritual. Earth and Water People may not be offended.

June 6, 1938

First day for ditch work & pertant ritual.

Pl. 97, a

PAINTING 80

Shichu Chief is holding the prayer stick and the War chiefs are sprinkling meal. *Kiama* (hill) in background.

During the 3 days' labor on the ditch in which all the men participate on pain of punishment, these chiefs, as well as the moiety chiefs, will remain in retreat, fasting and continent.

Ceremonialists are usually exempt from ditch work, originally, no doubt, because they were expected to engage at this time in ceremonial "work."

June 6, 1938

172

Kía ma →

Town Chief VI Chea Chea Kabick Kuamja war captain

putting pray" stick in middle of ditch before they begin to work

no 2

PAINTING 81

The moiety chiefs have also been in retreat and making prayer feathers which on the fourth morning they are "paying" to the Water People for the water they will let run through the ditch.

Black Eye Chief and his helpers are standing on the bank of the river where the irrigation ditch takes off. His helpers are throwing in seeds, ritual crops.

November 26, 1938

174

PAINTING 82

After the ritual at the ditch there is a procession back to town led by the Black Eye and Thliwa chiefs. The Thliwa chiefs "singing and saying yayu, yayu" are carrying turtle rattles, the rattles of the Black Eyes. Women, dancing and moving their arms up and down, go to meet the returning party.

Turtles are associated with the moieties, land turtle with the Red Eyes, water turtle with the Black Eyes. We recall that Thliwa dancers, like kachina dancers elsewhere, wear turtle-shell leg rattles. The grandfathers of the moiety groups are the ones who give permission to catch turtles.

November 26, 1938

176

PAINTING 83

After hearing the report of Black Eye Chief (he and his helpers are facing inward), Town Chief will thank him and all will pray together. Town Chief will give them permission to dance in "laplaza."

Formal reports and formal thanks for the reports are characteristic ceremonial manners among all Pueblos; chiefly permission to go or come and to hold dances or ceremonies seems peculiarly in vogue at Isleta, possibly also at Taos.

November 26, 1938

No 3.

PAINTING 8 4

Thliwa Chief is sixth from the right. Black Eye kapyo are bringing a Black Eye man to dance. Red Eye kapyo will bring Red Eye men and women.

Uwepör appears to be a fertility dance since *uwe* is said to describe a woman who has had many children. In English the dance is called Ditch Dance or Round Dance. The circle of alternating men and women holding hands moves antisunwise, twice around, until they complete the song.

The dance may be identical with the popular Round Dance of Taos which has some courtship significance. The Taos Round Dance is said to have been borrowed from the Utes and Sioux. However, a post-irrigation circle dance having the same Indian name as the Isletan dance is also performed by Keres, Tewa, and Towa.

November 26, 1938

180

uwepö fatility dance

Blak n Kopyo Taking this man to dance   If they refuse to go they Take them to Keam
                                          And them at Keam and Bring they back as they are not
No 4   And make them dance

PAINTING 85

Moiety kapyo serve not only as clowns but as police in ceremonial matters. The kapyo are temporarily appointed by the moiety chiefs and painted by them in the Round House.

If a person is remiss about joining in the dance, the kapyo will throw him into the river "for a swim and then bring him back and make him dance in his wet clothes." If relatives intervene before the river is reached and pray to the kapyo, giving them cigarettes and a cornhusk of cornmeal, the kapyo may let off the recalcitrant man or woman.

Ducking in punishment has been noted at Laguna and at Taos. Little boys were ducked at Zuni by bugaboo kachina and masked clowns. [Of course, anyone refusing to participate in the ditch work itself would be punished—today this usually takes the form of a fine (see French, 1948, p. 29).]

November 26, 1938

182

Yayayo Shaw

This man refuse to dance at v we put circle dance and taking him at Bury to Spare a serim Zher Shaw
him with stick on and bring him back and make him dance

No 5

PAINTING 86

After Uwepör the dancers withdraw into the kiva in dance procession, "dancing Kwarupör." *Kwaru* means weaving in and out in a zigzag; *pör* means dance.

January 23, 1939

184

no1

PAINTING 87

The racing season opens about the middle of March with the Town Chief's relay races for the Sun (Moon is represented by Shichu Chief). "The Town chief is going to clothe the Sun (give him prayer sticks) and help him run; that is why they run east and west." The permanent racetrack of Isleta and of all the Tanoans, "the road belonging to our Father Sun," lies east and west.

"The War chief (Kumpa) goes to the Town chief and asks him if it is time to race for the Sun. Then the Town chief gathers up his Kabewhiride (Bow chief) and Kumpa. They talk it over and Town chief sends Kabewhiride and the War chief (Kumpa) with the message to Shichukabede (All Colored Corn chief) at his house. There Shichu chief is sitting and thinking, and Kabewhiride will hand him a bundle of tobacco or meal and he will ask what word is sent him by the Town chief and when the day is to be. Shichu chief will thank them and say, 'I will call my helpers.' This will be Friday morning. The next morning they will begin to work at the Town chief's house. Shichu chief will place the altar and medicine bowl and sing and make prayer sticks to place at the racetrack Saturday night."

Note Shichu Chief's medicine box which contains batskin, feathers for prayer feathers, and, lying in cornmeal, animal figurines (kechu) and other stone fetishes (wahtainin, 'life people').

November 29, 1939

186

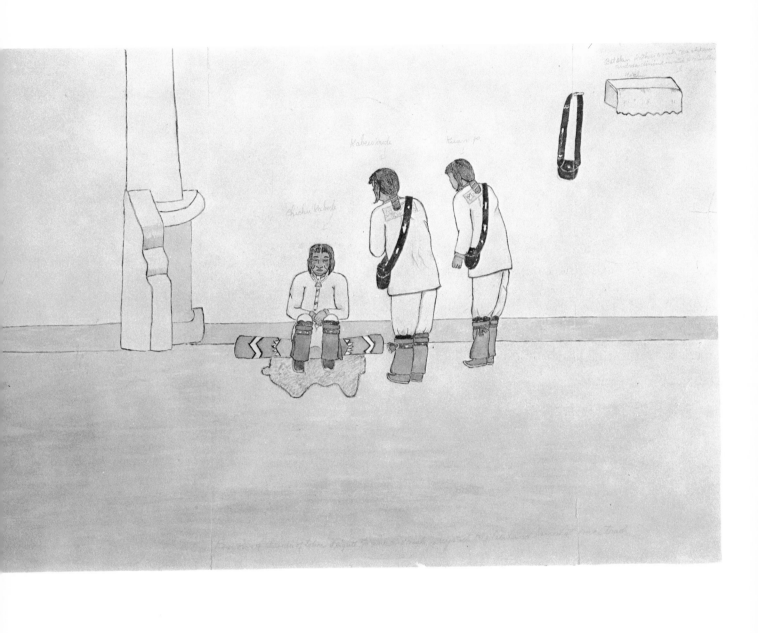

PAINTING 88

Shichu Chief has laid down the altar of Corn of All Colors, he being the Chief of one of the groups of varicolored corn, and in front of him lie feathers and turquoise beads, also cornhusks for smoking. The prayer sticks for the Sun were made before sunrise.

Note the "Salt Circle" which lies permanently on the floor of the Town Chief's ceremonial chamber.

November 29, 1939

188

PAINTING 89

War Chief (Kumpa) with bow and arrows, Shichu Chief with prayer stick, War Chief of the Cane and war captain are "paying the Sun for the race next day."

Depositing prayer sticks at night is unusual among Pueblos. Probably it is done in this case to insure secrecy, as the place of deposit is within the town. It would be consistent to plant a prayer stick for Moon at night, but not a prayer stick for Sun.

January 15, 1940

190

At midnight coming out to plant prayer sticks midway down trail

No 3

PAINTING 90

Shichu Chief's prayer stick is trimmed with turquoise and shell beads.

Night ritual outdoors is ever hazardous and should be well guarded, since witches are abroad by night. Both war chiefs—Kumpa "holding his bow and arrows and ritual stone" and the War Chief of the Cane—are present.[17]

---

[17] Note the stone cover of the pit. For its connection with irrigation cf. Lummis 1920, p. 165, and Wittfogel and Goldfrank, 1943, p. 24, note 55.—ESG.

January 15, 1940

192

Placing prayer stick in middle of Race Track at night night

No 4

PAINTING 91

The day after the race, Shichu Chief will perform his ceremonial in the house of the Town Chief. He will make medicine water and lay his altar. It is the function of the women members of his chieftaincy to bring him water from the river early in the morning. This is a regular function of women members of such groups.

February 12, 1940

194

PAINTING 9 2

From early morning until noon while Shichu Chief is at work at his altar set up in Town Chief's house, War Chief with his bow, arrows, and stone knife sits guard on the roof. When the work is finished they will tell him to come down. They will all smoke and give thanks to the War Chief for his service.

In the afternoon Shichu people will come and get their drink of medicine water, and at this time infants may be brought in to get their Shichu Corn name.

February 12, 1940

196

PAINTING 93

Shichu Chief's medicine water drunk by the runners and sprinkled on them will render them "strong in the race and protect them from harm." (Black magic is sometimes used during the race.)

From the Town Chief's house with a rear guard of two war captains, the runners will go singing to the Round House where Town Chief, War Chief (Kumpa), and Corn group chiefs are waiting for them. They will halt at the hatch and sing their ritualistic race songs, "asking permission of Wadinin [wahtainin?] to enter. The chiefs inside say, 'Come in, my sons, come in, my sons.' "

June 1940

198

PAINTING 94

On the third and last Sunday of Town Chief's races, early before people arrive, Shichu Chief sprays medicine water—"holy water," writes Felipe—on Round House, ladder, posts, and fire screen, around wall horns, and into the pit of the wahtainin, the spirit people, he pours a little. Meanwhile his assistant prays.

Then "they" circle around the kiva, and "come up on the west side and go out on the east side. Then the fire man comes down to build the fire."

June 23, 1941

200

no 5.

PAINTING 9 5

At noon a war captain calls out for the race and in some years, before the race, for a war dance (cf. Painting 97), saying "Father, brothers, all who are around come to the kiva [Round House] with faith and good cheer."

January 15, 1940

202

PAINTING 96

The War Chief gets the runners going with a push of his bow. The tree marks the starting point. The jar contains medicine water for the thirsty.

The Town Chief's races for Sun and Moon are followed by a race by Corn groups, but with less ritual and with betting.

At Zuni the spring kick-race calendar is somewhat similar: a ritual War Society race to open with and secular betting races afterward. There is also racing by clan. Kick-racing among Hopi is by kiva or clan, without betting.

Hopi and Zuni clan racers are painted with a clan design or glyph, perhaps the closest approach Pueblos made to writing. Note the cross painted on the chest of the Isletan Corn group (pseudo-clan) runner.

November 2, 1936

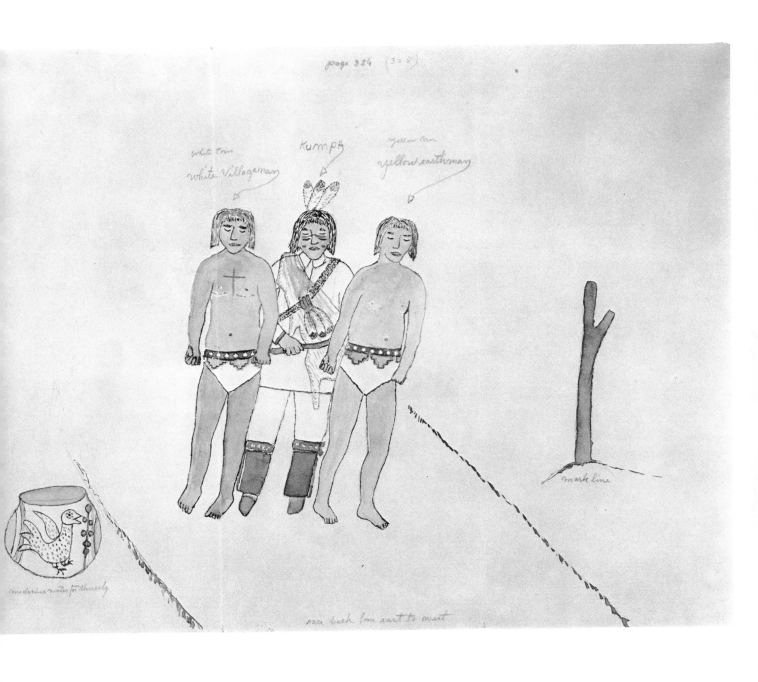

white man
white Villageman

Kumpa

yellow man
yellow earthman

medicine water for thirsty

mark line

race back from east to west

PAINTING 97

Racing and war are conceptually and ceremonially related by the Pueblos. As noted above, at Isleta on the day of a race, a war dance may be performed as well as a scalp ritual in the Round House where the scalps are kept and where offerings are made to the Navaho dead. Some years at this time also, the return of the war party is dramatized, as in this painting (see Parsons, 1932, pp. 325 ff.).

With the scalp wrapped in a whole buckskin, these representatives of successful raiders have spent the night camping outside the town. Besides the scalp bundle on the back of the leader, who is inferably the Bow Chief (Kabew'iride),[18] a ceremonial quiver and a shield are carried. On the west side four little fires have been built. Before approaching the Round House the raiders pass between the smoking fires in order "to blind and weaken more Navaho so it will be easy killing next time."

Rabbits are similarly blinded (Painting 115), but before the hunt, not afterward. Possibly the war raid smokes were once thought of as exorcism by fumigation—fumigation of scalp or scalpers.

As the five men approach the Round House they sing and call like a coyote—"hu! hu! hu!"

This return-from-war dramatization has lapsed. Felipe is describing merely from hearsay.

---

[18] As noted above, the succession to the Town Chieftaincy was considerably disturbed in the last decades of the 19th century, and there is evidence of changing (and merged) ceremonial functions. The artist never saw the Scalp Dance. Lummis, who died in 1891, commented that the scalps were carried by the Mapuride (see Parsons, 1932, p. 327, note 44a, and commentary to Painting 98), and the account given by Dr. Parsons in Isleta, N. Mex. (pp. 326 ff.) continually emphasizes the leading role, not of Kabew'iride, but, as could be expected, of Kumpa, the permanent War Chief, the head of the War Society, and the guardian of the scalps. Moreover, the ceremonial quiver which is the property of the Kabew'iride is, according to the artist, loaned by him to Kumpa only during the hunt ceremonial (cf. Painting 117). However, in view of the close conceptual relation between hunting and war, it is conceivable that Kumpa carries this quiver in the Scalp Dance as well. Enough here to draw attention to the conflicting data. Further inquiry alone can resolve the confusion.—ESG.

May 5, 1941

PAINTING 98

Early in the morning, 4 days after the entrance of the returning "warriors," there is a victory dance. To start the dance the Bow Chief (Kabew'iride) who is the assistant and successor of the Town Chief carries the scalp bundle and with the ceremonial quiver leads in the *Mapuride* and the War Chief of the Cane.

The Mapuride wears a Hopi woman's blanket and the big boots of the Taos woman. She is called "the bending one," according to Lummis (1908, p. 241), because she carries the scalps on her back. Felipe represents the Bow Chief with the scalps on his back and, in the dance, the Mapuride holding a scalp pole. Felipe has never seen a proper scalp dance. "They still have the war dance but they don't use the scalps now."

May 5, 1941

208

PAINTING 99

Four rows, two outer rows of women, two inner rows of men. The men carrying bow, arrows, and quiver, and with feathers in their hair are War Society members; the men with guns are the warriors. Dancing to and fro between the lines is the Mapuride, as she formerly held the scalp pole. The faces of all the men are painted. Mapuride's forehead and the lower part of her face are painted white and red, a red spot on cheek and, like the Taos Bear Mother, black from corner of mouth to temple.

June 23, 1941

210

War dance.   No 2

PAINTING 100

After they dance and sing around the plaza, the scalp dancers withdraw into the Round House to rest and practice. One War Society man remains as "watchman for the scalp." Each time they come up from the kiva the watchman unfastens the pole from the ladder and passes it to the Mapuride, bidding her to have a strong heart and take care of the Navaho. "I take the pole," says the Mapuride, and forth they go to repeat their dance procession.

June 23, 1941

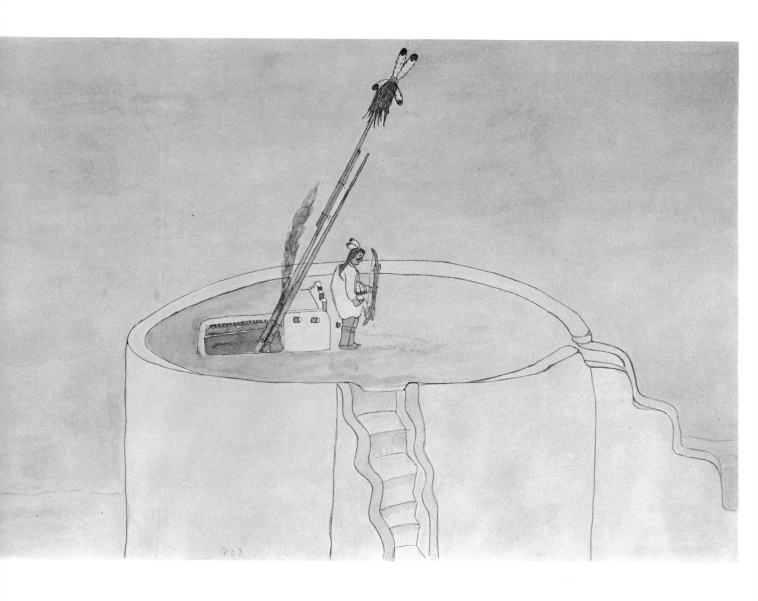

No. 3.

PAINTING 101

The *Mapurnin* are biting the scalps and spewing into a bowl to make medicine mud cakes which will be wrapped in cornhusks. (Note the basket of mud and cornhusks.)

This scalp medicine is handed over to the Town Chief, who will assign it to medicine men for sick persons or "worry people," to strengthen them and give them power. Inferably, the Mapurnin make this medicine in the Round House when the dramatic scalp ceremony is under way.

The regular duties of the two Mapurnin are to feed the scalps in the Round House and to clean the Round House—they are the only women allowed to do this. The War Chief (Kumpa) is the manager of the Round House and the Mapurnin are his "Mothers." It is also the function of the Mapuride to clean the racetrack before the race that is run in connection with the scalp ceremony.

November 2, 1936

214

page 327

PAINTING 102

Early in the morning of the race—about 4 a.m.—the Mapuride goes to the east end of the racetrack where the race starts, casts pollen to the Sun, prays, and begins to sweep. She faces west and may not sweep backward or turn backward; she must face the west until she finishes.

As soon as she begins to sweep, the wives of the War Society men go out to help. When they have all reached the west end of the track, about sunrise, the Mapuride stands and prays, thanking her helpers and telling them that "they have earned long life from their Father Sun."

A special broom made of tall plants is used on this occasion.

June 23, 1941

216

PAINTING 103

When a member of the War Society or even one higher up "makes a mistake they punish him in the Town Chief's house. They mark the floor with cornmeal and place the Kumpa [or the errant individual] with his toes to the mark and facing west, and he has to stay the way they place him. They say he is being punished by the gods from all the directions, east, north, west, south, and middle. [Note the lines of the directions.] They leave a watchman [another member of the War Society] to watch him; in case he falls the watchman gets him up. As long as he sits there he has to sing their secret songs until the Chief of the War society says to excuse him. Maybe all day or night he stays there. Then after he is forgiven by the Chief they sing, and the [guilty] man begins to cry. After that he can hardly walk; he may be crippled or lame for a few days. This punishment they call biedakuer [*Paidekore = paide*, War chief, *makore*, circle]."

Rio Grande Keres refer to this punishment as seating or standing a person in the circle. It is dreaded. [For Cochiti, cf. Dumarest, 1919, p. 201.]

April 8, 1941

218

P A I N T I N G   1 0 4

The day before planting, the women shell corn from the biggest ear saved from the past crop and of the color they want. They place it in a large basket or bowl; they chew a root called *ballafia* and spit it over the seed. In the morning the man who intends to plant comes in singing, "Weide, may my corn come out of the ground forthwith like the tail of the roadrunner or like the tail of the red bird!" Still singing he picks up the bag of seed. A woman hiding outside with a jar of water from the river will pour water (and suds) on the man as he starts out. The women inside get water in a gourd dipper and also sprinkle him, to bring rain as soon as the field is planted.

February 12, 1940

noi O.

PAINTING 105

In June a rain ceremony, "rain fast," is performed by the Town Chief, the chiefs of both medicine societies, and the two war chiefs (Kumpa and War Chief of the Cane). The chiefs are in retreat 12 days. The medicine chiefs are believed to go long distances "by their power" and clean the springs. The last night of the ceremony is public, but women rarely attend because they are fearful of the manifestations of thunder and lightning which are said to occur in the ceremonial chamber.

The Corn groups go into retreat from June 5 to 15, closing with the Shichu ceremony and a Kachina Night Dance.

November 1936

222

Kumpa

medicine man

war chief

page 330. Rain Ceremony

PAINTING 106

San Agostín is the patron saint of Isleta. His fiesta is celebrated on August 28; but his help may be needed earlier, say in June, from the 20th to the 25th, in case of drought. In the early Spanish way he will be shown his duty.

After a Mass paid for by the townspeople "they take Father Sangustin, old man Augustin, out to the fields to give us a rain after he sees that the fields are dry and need rain on a hot day. If a woman is sick she will promise if she gets well that on that day she will go barefoot, with no shade, nothing on head, as you see the one carrying the saint. The men carry a shotgun to shoot up into the air every once in a while. One man goes in front with a cross followed by a boy ringing a bell once in a while. The men carry the shade and the women carry the saint, only women, no men. The last man is the Lieutenant Governor, who is in charge to keep the people together, to see that no one drops behind, that they stay together."

November 14, 1939

the women promise that day to like she is
no abse on

no 1
Carrying of man over field for train
Saint Augustine's

PAINTING 107

Writes Felipe: "On returning from the fields they bring old man Augustin to the Governor's house and dance, as you see them. They always set two small cotton trees side by side and they make a shade of cotton-tree branches. Two men stand guard with a gun on each side of the saint. They keep two men there all day long, not one minute do they leave the saint without these guards until he is taken back to his place on the church altar. And a woman is always behind the saint lest he fall. He might jump if he did not like something, bad thoughts. They dance all afternoon."

Note the pointing up gesture of one of the choir, probably here as elsewhere a rain gesture.

November 14, 1939

226

No 2.
Dancing for Saint Augustine at Governor House.

PAINTING 108

In Spanish America an overnight *velorio,* a wake, for a saint is a familiar practice, often in fulfillment of a vow, as Felipe describes. "A woman has promised to take Our Mother Virgin, Kekei Virken, into her house. She has fixed the place up, as you see, decorated with blanket and handkerchiefs. It is called an altar. She has placed Our Mother on the table and will keep her all night 'til daylight. They all keep awake. As you see, as she has promised, a woman is putting a handkerchief on Our Mother's back as women wear them. This saint has many beads and hand-kerchiefs paid her by those who have promised them, and she has all of them on her back. For long, long years she has been getting presents. The women promise only to this Mother Virgin; men promise to old man Augustin. The woman who has promised to keep the saint all night at this velorio will have to carry the saint from the church to her house and then back to the church. Her relatives will help."

The other woman is just visiting the saint.

November 14, 1939

228

The palace is decorated →

Mother Virgin

Visiting the Saint

She is placing hand kerchief at Mother Virgin

no 3.
Mother Virgin at womans home

PAINTING 109

This dance is called *Pinitu* (Spruce) Kachina Dance.

Spruce is the tree of the kachina; it grows in their mountain homes, is used as trim for kachina dancers, and is associated with the clowns who attend the kachina. Generally, spruce is fetched the day before the dance.

In the picture we see the moiety kapyo clowns bringing spruce in for the autumn kachina dance. They bring in two whole trees, for the clowns to gather around, one for the Black Eye clowns, one for the Red Eye clowns. The clowns have been appointed, but they have not yet been "made," i.e., painted, in the Round House.

November 1936

230

332. bringing wood from mountain on dancing eve, there are tupid line they are painted

PAINTING 110

The kapyo clowns have been painted by the moiety chiefs in the Round House and are coming out to "play," as the Zuni would say.

June 15, 1936

232

PAINTING 111

One of the "play" acts of the kapyo clowns is a marriage farce. The head kapyo seats the others, one by one, in the "house" (those who are under the trees are waiting their turn) and with each he carries on the following colloquy: "Do you want to get married?"—"No."—"You should get married. You are old enough."—"All right. I will marry."—"You want to get married, but you cannot work. Whom will you marry?" The oldest woman in town may be named. After the "bridegroom" is assigned his house he is told how to behave as a married man—humor reflecting several social standards of conduct.

December 3, 1937

234

this where they dance on North side

Papy getting many

PAINTING 112

Before this "play," the clowns, two by two, have made the rounds of the houses of their "aunts" to tell them to prepare bread, rabbits, and turtles, and also chili, watermelons, bowls, calico, etc. These "gifts" are then carried to the "houses" where the clowns will eat.

Eating outdoors is characteristic of Pueblo clowns. So is the present-giving function of paternal kinswomen. Compare the picture of "aunts" bringing food to their "nephews" among Hopi of First Mesa (Parsons, 1939, pl. 15), and also the picture of their father's clanswomen, bringing food bowls to the koyemshi clowns of Zuni (Stevenson, 1904, pl. 68).

December 3, 1937

236

no 2

This are aunts Ityumin

PAINTING 1 1 3

The next day there is to be a rabbit hunt and the clowns will be in charge. After sleeping in the Round House they dance at sunrise on the rooftops on the four sides of the plaza. When the people see them they begin to get ready for the hunt.

Note the terrace cloud design found not only among Pueblos but in pre-Inca and pre-Aztec civilizations.

November 1936

238

sheafume 6   6 Shure

stage
dry for hunting

line on 65

PAINTING 114

The next evening, before the hunt, the hunters sing all night to the drum, and in the middle of their circle they keep a little fire going to weaken and blind the rabbits. They plan where in the hills they will meet. At this *nawah* the war captain gives permission to anyone to beat the drum, to any old man who knows the songs. The war captain has asked for the drum from Black Eye Chief or Red Eye Chief. He asks for the drum with a prayer and gives the Chief a cigarette. The drum is called Thunder Sound Man. It is made with ritual and prayed to at dances, as in the Zuni Scalp Dance and among Yaqui Indians, and probably elsewhere.

In this painting the war captain (in a pink striped shirt) is seated between the fire and the house.

June 14, 1939

Was Bptow

Corshug's Slano.

mawah

In the case of Rabbit hunt in Spots as described of dance.

No. 4.

PAINTING 115

While the hunters are in the hills, singing and drumming and keeping a fire going to weaken and blind the rabbits, the Hunt Chief holds a ceremony in his own house to which only War chiefs, war captains, the head kapyo, and Corn chiefs may be admitted. Hunt Chief is sitting between two helpers behind the altar. War Chief (of the Cane) and captains to their right and in front. One war captain is rolling a cigarette for Hunt Chief to smoke to song and blow the smoke in the direction of the hunt hill in order to blind the rabbits. War Chief (Kumpa) sits to the left of the Hunt Chief and beyond him sit the three head kapyo. The fetishes on the altar are Hunt Chief's stone figurines of Wolf [cf. Titiev, 1944, p. 157, note 17; Woodbury, 1954, pp. 161 f.]. Note also the stone points and the War Chief's bow and arrows in his ceremonial mountain lion skin quiver [see commentary to Painting 117].

All night long, until daylight, they work and sing to blind the rabbits. Compare the Shoshonean hunt shaman who captures the souls of game animals so that the game animals wander helplessly (Steward, 1938, p. 34).

July 29, 1939

242

PAINTING 116

In the morning, after their night "work," preparations for the hunt fire are begun.

A ritual rabbit hunt fire is made by all the Pueblos, and its function is generally said to be to blind and bewilder the rabbits.

July 29, 1937

after work   Next day taking action from True Chief house To hills to start fire for hunting.

PAINTING 117

Alongside the Hunt Chief lies his "little wolf pouch" containing his wolf figurines.
Throughout the hunt ceremonial the War Chief is on guard. He carries a lion
hide quiver which belongs to Kabewʻiride but is used only for this ceremonial [cf.
p. 206, note 18]. "The lion has power to draw game," writes Felipe, "because the lion
himself is a hunter." Among other Pueblos, Mountain Lion, rather than Wolf, is the
patron spirit of hunting.

July 29, 1939

246

The hunt Chief building fire at hill.

PAINTING 118

Now some of the hunters have arrived. Note their curved throwing stick *(koa)*, which is a club rather than the curved, boomeranglike stick used in the Western Pueblos and by the ancient people.

At Red Sand Hill (see commentary to Painting 31) the unbaptized children are deposited, and it is also reputed to be a stopping place of witches.

July 29, 1939

At Name Koto

The Rabbit hunter Gathering waiting till they all come together with hunt Chief & war Chief

PAINTING 119

It is or was customary among the Pueblos for the women to go out on some of the rabbit drives, usually, if not always, the drives asked for by the Kachina organization. The women go on foot. They will run up to a man who has made a kill, and he will give the rabbit to the woman who reaches him first.

At Isleta the women go by wagon or horseback—Tiwa women and, among Pueblos, only Tiwa women ride horses. On the first drive or encirclement the hunters give the Hunt Chief all their rabbits and he gives them to the women. After that the women run after anyone who gets a rabbit.

The last wagon carries barrels of water. A war captain is in the lead as guard.

March 10, 1939

250

PAINTING 120

In his left hand, the man in the lead carries a stone wolf fetish belonging to the Hunt Chief.

The kapyo clowns figure in this hunt, as they did in the Hunt Chief's night ceremony. Elsewhere also the clown groups are associated with rabbit drives, particularly those connected with kachina dances. These are also the "hunts with the girls."

The clowns are carrying the willow branches associated with them, red willow by the Black Eyes, yellow willow by the Red Eyes.

March 10, 1939

252

PAINTING 121

In return for the rabbits they are receiving from the Hunt Chief, the women will repay him the next day with tortillas and a bowl of rabbit stew.

March 10, 1939

254

Hunt Rabbit

no 3.

PAINTING 122

Hunt Chief will drag the rabbit around the circle five times; then he will pray in all directions to Wolf, the Master of Game. In his hand he holds his wolf fetish. War Chief stands on guard.

August 13, 1939

markstan chief

Hanos

Hunt Chief

The very first one Rabbit is kill and hunt chief making circl marking ground he is singing

No1.

PAINTING 123

The Hunt Chief "lays the rabbit head to the east. He is singing as he tears with one rip each ear and hand and foot. This means that he is sending the rabbit with a mark to the great Hunt Chief (Wolf), wherever he may be—east, north, west, south, or in the middle."

Here is a kind of blood or animal offering unique among contemporary Pueblos.

August 13, 1939

258

He turn Rabbt in all direction telling the name of direction and bye. Rabbts head part split open saro face and feet too

No2

PAINTING 124

Late in the day and after having eaten, Hunt Chief and War Chief leave the hunters and return to the hunt fire where "the Hunt chief locked up all rabbits in a circle by his power." As he sings he keeps moving the arrow east, north, west, and south, making a cross. As soon as the ashes are spread out he will, he thinks, have freed the rabbits from his power.

August 13, 1939

maschief 7

Ashes where he had fire   hunt theif

In even returning Come back where he start fire and singing & jim making Croos this means he is sleepy Poor

NO 3.

Pette o

PAINTING 125

Before describing the kachina dances to which the foregoing rabbit hunt and ritual are incidental, it may not be inappropriate to indicate the ceremonial treatment of a dead deer. (For ritual before and during a deer hunt, see Parsons, 1932, pp. 337-338).

The deer is laid out with head toward the sun and covered with a woman's *manta* because the deer's hide is to be given to a woman to be used for her voluminous puttee moccasins. Beads are hung around the deer's neck and a string of prayer feathers are stretched from antler to antler.

Every visitor to the hunter's house will draw "breath" from the dead deer, as one war captain is doing, and will sprinkle meal from a basket, as the other war captain is doing. To the Town Chief and Hunt Chief and to all his relatives the hunter will give a piece of venison. "That means you will have luck and get more deer."

May 16, 1939

P A I N T I N G   1 2 6

Now we turn to the Thliwa dances. Early in the morning of the Thliwa *Kompör* they have to get ready. A little boy is painted as Aiyayaode by Black Eye Chief. "No one else is allowed to paint him. He has to be made by their [Black Eye] hand and power, no one is allowed in the private room where he is made. The Black Eye chief will tell the Chakabede [the Thliwa Chief] about the work for little Aiyayaode, about this Aiyayaode ceremonial. Chakabede must have a good heart and [good] thoughts and he must preach this to all the dancers. Little Aiyayaode will never stand still. In the picture he is pretending to kneel down on one leg and he is raising his arm just as he will do dancing with the Thliwale, he will keep on the move."

Another little Aiyayaode is painted by the Red Eye Chief to dance with the Red Eye dancers.

According to a previous informant (Parsons, 1932), Aiyayaode represents Wildcat, who at the Emergence opened up the way from underground. In San Juan mythology Wildcat has a similar role.

April 18, 1939

Chatchecedy   Blacheyicheif.   Anyayaode.

PAINTING 127

Thliwa Chief stands at the head of the line.

Four days in the moiety kivas the two sets of dancers, Black Eyes and Red Eyes, have been practicing. During this time they sleep in their respective kivas (continence is required), but they do not need to remain continuously in retreat.

The sets alternate, dancing at each appearance on all sides of the plaza in an antisunwise circuit. This alternating dance pattern is also typical of the two-kiva system of Rio Grande Keres and Tewa.

November 1936

266

a'yaya'de

page 335 Frame 23

PAINTING 128

These bundles, "the thliwa bags that keep the power" [*waiide tainin*, as Felipe writes it, or Life People], the drums, Aiyayaode cap, and grandfather masks are kept in the moiety kivas, one set for the Black Eyes, one set for the Red Eyes. "The chief and his helper take turns going to the kiva every morning to say hakuwam (greetings) at the door and go in and pray."

The big bowl is kept full of water "as all these things might want to drink. The little window is to see the Sun when they fast."

This picture is satisfactory evidence that the Isleta Thliwa and the grandfather clowns are directly connected with the moiety organization.

February 3, 1939

268

PAINTING 129

Alone—"just as he [Haukabede] came out from under the earth alone, carrying little gourds." His face is painted white and in his hair are prayer feathers, such as are worn by a medicine man.

Formerly on the night or nights of Thliwa dancing (either Thliwapör or Thliwa Kompör, it is uncertain), there was also a dance called *Helele*. This belonged to Haukabede. The last Haukabede, a man named Hakamito, died several years ago, and after his death the dance ceremonial lapsed. The office could be filled only by the Town Chief, and as the Town Chief, the last "real" Town Chief, died before Hakamito died, the office of Haukabede has remained vacant. One break in Pueblo ceremonialism often involves another break.

Like the Town Chief, Haukabede worked for the Sun. As he "came up" with little gourds he was probably associated with primitive farming. If Haukabede was the counterpart of the Keresan Town chief associate (Tshraikatsi, see p. 10, note 12) his function was to increase the supply of plants and game. *Hau* means to be replete— *haukabede*, 'supply chief.'

August 31, 1939

270

ha'u Kabele

Ba'wa chi
presbiaben
lik. hurdan
men

painted white ba...

Goasla

no1

PAINTING 130

The notched-stick players *(komnin)* have been asked to play by Haukabede, with prayer and a cigarette. They will play for the Helele dancers and for *Thliwalepör,* but *not* for the Shichu Dance (here the reference seems to be to Thliwapör, and the presence of the grandfathers would tend to confirm this).

Each player carries his turkey-tail headdress, gourd, notched stick *(kom)*, and deer-leg scraper.

August 3, 1939

272

PAINTING 131

Helele was performed as part of Haukabede's "work" for the Sun. He and the members of the War Society (Kumpawithlawen) sing to the notched-stick playing. Below sits the fire tender. A woman is bringing the singers a bowl of sirup. Nearby sits *Tochide*, Chief of the White Corn People, the "White Earth Day people." The Chief of the Yellow Corn People, the Earth People, sits smoking against the pillar.

The grandfathers will join in the dance to make people laugh and shorten the time. Dancing continues all through the night. There are many more onlookers than are represented here.

August 31, 1939

274

No 3.

PAINTING 132

The gourd resonators lie on a buffalo hide.

Notched-stick playing has a wide distribution among Indian tribes. Among Pueblos the notched stick accompanies several kachina dances. Sometimes the players impersonate women, possibly because sometimes the playing may represent corn grinding. At Isleta the players are associated with war (insofar as the War Society sings), with hunting (deer-leg scraper, buffalo hide), and with farming since they scrape for the Thliwa and for a chief associated with agriculture. If this chief was once in charge of the sacred "nest" in the Town Chief's house he was also associated with game animals. (See p. 10, note 12, and commentary to Painting 33.)

August 31, 1939

PAINTING 133

On October 10, 15, and 20, the War Society members bring in corn from all the fields, one ear from each field, to the Town Chief, first burying another ear, one of the largest and best, in each cornfield as an offering to *Nam Thliu*, Earth Old Woman, or, as Felipe writes, "old mother ground"—"feeding her, thanking, and paying her for raising the corn and asking her to grow more next year."

September 13, 1939

PAINTING 134

On October 10, the War Society members bring in the corn from fields on the south side; on October 15, from fields on the north side; on October 20, from fields on the east side, one ear of corn from each field. "This means that they open the road to the people to gather their corn. You see the Town chief has to get it first. Then the Crier goes to the ash piles and hollers, giving permission to the people to gather their corn." The War Society members go out early in the morning "around 3 or 4 o'clock"; they come in about noon.

On each side of town there is an ash pile where offerings are made to Weide and the dead. [Also of interest here is the demonstrated connection between war and fertility.]

October 13, 1939

280

All Kwampas

They go early in morning around 3 n a they come in about noon.
Kwampa bring corn from all corn field to town Chief Emmanuel house.
No one can gather corn before this

PAINTING 135

As the woman puts out the food, she calls her dead father, mother, brother, or sister by name to come out and eat.

On November 1, the Day of the Dead, at noon, in their own houses "the ladies cut foods of different kinds and mix them; they place it all in a middle room where no one can see; a plate for each deceased member of the family. They keep the candles burning from the time they begin to place the food. If a candle burns out, they replace it with another. The candles burn all night until next day at noon. The following night they take the candles out on the hill and bury them."

The Snake Father who cured his kinswoman of toothache was remembered this way by his relatives on the *Dia de Todos Santos*. At any time this powerful medicine man could be asked to cure or give what is wanted, like a saint.

Pueblos, like Mexican Indians, celebrate both days, All Saints' (November 1) and All Souls' (November 2), as the days of the dead. (In Mexico the first day is for the dead children of the family, the second day for the dead adults.)

November 29, 1939

PAINTING 136

The next day, November 2, "the ladies take their *responsos (thliachia)* to their family graves and place them there: corn or bread in middle of corn in big bowls." They keep candles burning until noon, when at the graves the priest sprinkles the bowls with holy water. Then the women take the bowls to the priest's residence where he piles the bread to sell to Mexicans.

"These two days the bell will ring once every little while. The first day it begins to ring after 12 o'clock and rings all the afternoon. It rests at night, then starts the next morning to ring until noon. Then it is over."

November 29, 1939

284

Women place their food and candles family, on father's grave.

Responsor.

Graves at church yard.

No 2.   Second day at Grave.

PAINTING 137

Catholic ritual is over, but not aboriginal ritual, for the night of All Souls',
November 2, in the dark, women again visit the graves. They dig a little hole at the
head of each grave, place food in it and fill up the hole. "Then the woman feels
happy for she feels the dead is eating her food; she is feeding the dead."

They break the bowl and leave it on top. "Any bowl or dish used for dead person
they always break up so no one can use it."

January 6, 1941

286

putting food on head

↓ head

stone →

feeding a dead person on grave where he or she is buried

after funeral they make cross on top with stones

PAINTING 138

The White Corn people and the Blue Corn people (possibly each Corn group) possess a crudely anthropomorphic stone fetish, which is placed on the altar.

Hakabatö (A) belonging to the Day or White Corn people, "a woman made of rock" was "found that way in the east," the direction associated with the group.

For the comparable fetish of Blue Corn People *(B)* I have no specific name.

These figurines belong, I think, among the wahtainin. [Cf. stone fetish belonging to head of Hopi Bear clan described in Titiev, 1944, pp. 66 ff.]

A, December 3, 1937; B, January 20, 1938

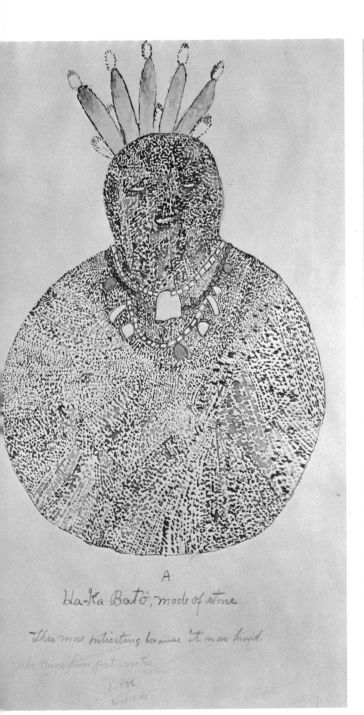

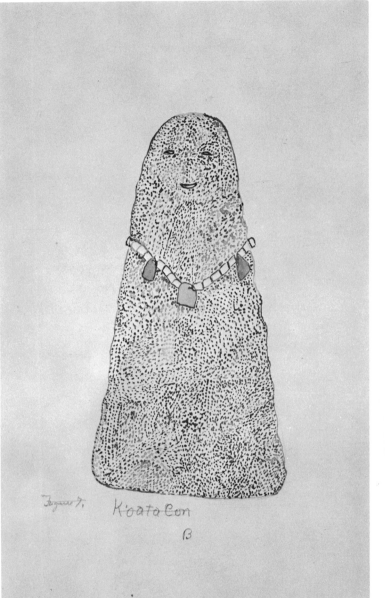

A

Hla-Ka Batö, mode of stone

This more intresting because it was kind.
who tens from patc cetse

8-576
East side

Figure 7,   K'oataeon

B

PAINTING 139

Besides these anthropomorphic altar stones there are fetish or spirit stones in shrines, as among the Tewa and at Taos. Compare the Stone Men in the mountain shrine of Taos.

Before setting out to hunt, trade, or travel, an Isletan always goes to *Hiothliute*, Stone Old Woman, and asks "this Stone old woman to give him what he is going after or for good luck on his way" [cf. Dumarest, 1919, pp. 206 f., and picture of a seemingly similar shrine in Goldfrank, 1927, p. 71].

December 25, 1940

290

Stone old lady
L Rio Liso

praying and asking what he need or want,
paying with meal and turquoise

704

PAINTING 140

Prayer sticks *(natoai)* and prayer feathers *(thlawashie, thlawa* = fringe; *shie,* tied ?):

1. For Water People, from any Corn group or medicine man, although different feathers are used by different groups.
2. For springs, from Black Eyes, on fetching spruce. The feathers, upper center, are sparrow hawk and yellow bird; lower center, duck; left side (facing), eagle; right side (facing), turkey. Paints are red *(pire)* and blue kofanta, possibly malachite.
3. For springs, from Red Eyes, on fetching spruce. Upper center, humming bird and blue jay *(koalakide);* lower center, duck; left side, turkey; right side, upper, eagle; lower, turkey.
4. For the Sun, from Town Chief. Three eagle feathers, bluebird, red bird, roadrunner, duck. Beads and turquoise.
5. For the Moon, from Town Chief. Three eagle feathers, yellow bird, duck, roadrunner, Red beads.
6. For the dead. Different Corn groups use different feathers, the feathers of birds belonging to the group of the deceased. For a Goose Corn group they will use a goose feather. They use the feather of duck, bluebird or of any little bird belonging to the group. These feathers are kept lying on the floor.

Prayer sticks and prayer feathers are used among other Pueblos except the northern Tiwa, who employ only prayer feathers.

January 15, 1940

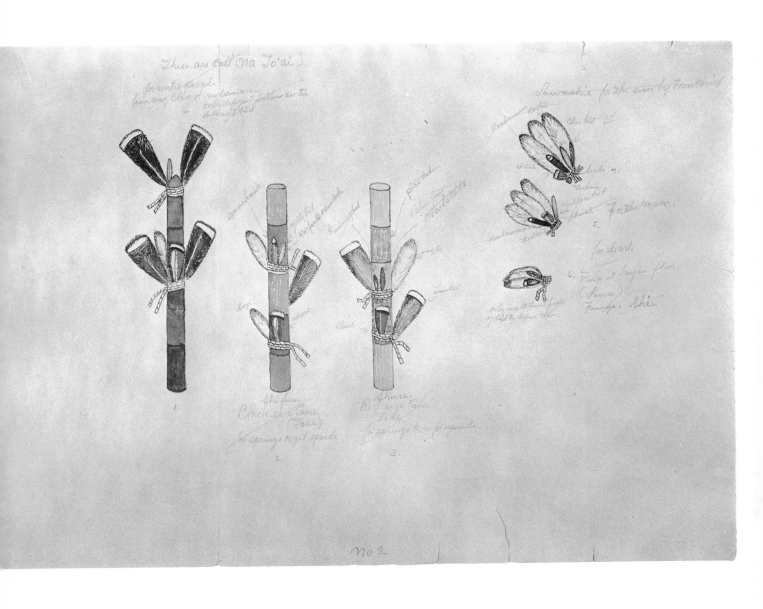

ANNOTATED GLOSSARY OF ISLETA TERMS

By George L. Trager

When Elsie Clews Parsons first arranged the material in the present book, she asked the compiler of this glossary to check the linguistic form of the native words she wanted to include. The writer had at that time a not too long Isleta vocabulary in his possession (collected in 1935), and by using that and extrapolating from his extensive Taos materials he was able to send Dr. Parsons on October 1, 1940, a considerable list of identifications of words. That list is on cards which are now in the archives of the Bureau of American Ethnology, cataloged No. 4540-A.

The editor of the present work asked the compiler for further checking early in 1959; since the latter had done a little additional fieldwork on Isleta in 1957, and had greatly extended his Taos material in the intervening years, he was able to revise and correct the list in many places, as well as to bring the orthography into line with his present usage. (It may be noted that the phonological correspondences between Taos and Isleta have been worked out—see G. L. Trager, "The historical phonology of the Tiwa languages," Studies in Linguistics, vol. 1, No. 5 (10 pp.), 1942—and it is easy to arrive at the correct Isleta form of a word cognate with a known Taos word.) In the summer of 1959, during tenure of a National Science Foundation grant to investigate paralanguage in Taos, the compiler was able to spend a few hours with his original Isleta informant, and check over the whole of the list below and record it, with all questions and commentary, on tape. This resulted in a number of significant corrections and additional identifications. But it must be emphasized that there are still unidentified items, and that many of the identifications are uncertain, either in meaning or in some aspect of the linguistic form; extensive general fieldwork on the language would be required to correct this.

The glossary is arranged in alphabetical order of the terms recorded by Dr. Parsons. After the term, a linguistically correct version is given, in the following orthography:

vowels—i, e, a, u, ə; į, ę, ą, ų, ə̨; ie, əa, ua; įę, ə̨ą, ųą

consonants—p, t, k, kw; p', t', k'; ph, th, kh; c [č], c'; ł, s, š, h, hw; m, n, y, w, r

accents, etc.—middle tone primary stress ´, medial stress `; high tone primary ˝, medial ˇ; low tone primary ˆ, medial ˵; weak stress unmarked; internal open transition (juncture) shown by +

In the cards made in 1940, kw and hw were written as kʷ, hʷ; ph, th, kh as pʽ, tʽ, kʽ; y as j; ʼ asˈ;ˋas ₁; ʺ and ˇ as ʼ; ^ and ˮ as ˈ; + was not shown.

After the rewritten form there is a translation in single quotation marks, and in many instances there is some linguistic analysis of the term by stems and affixes, and additional comment. Doubtful items are indicated by question marks; '?' means 'meaning unknown'.

Aiya: ?

Aiyayaho: ? 'àyay'ə́w ('ayay- ?, 'ə́w- 'boy')

Aiyayaode: ? 'àyay'ə́wde ('ayay- ?, 'ə́wde 'boy')

akuam machede him kaa waean 'greetings, come in, my fathers': 'ak'ûwäˈm mạcə́ad, 'imkhà'a+wẽ̂'in ('a- 'you', k'û- 'good', wâm 'live' = '[may] you live well, greetings'; mạ- 'you' plural, cə́ad 'come in, enter'; 'im- 'our', khá'a- 'father', wẽ̂'in 'those who are')

akuamhura machead 'greetings, come in': 'ak'ûwäm, mạcə́ad as in previous entry, -hura ?

awa shie ukoweje 'you life (stone) knife may you be old': 'awä̀šíe 'ukə́awẽ̀cě 'may you have a long life' ('a- 'your', wâ- 'life', šíe 'stoneknife', 'u- 'you', kə́awẽ̀cě '[you] will be old' = 'may you be old [by] your life-knife')

ballafia: pàrɫä̀+phíe 'food(?)-big-root'

biedakuer [paideköre = paide war chief, maköre circle] 'a form of punishment': ? p'ä̀'íde '?', khə́ri 'circle'

Chakabede: càkạbéde 'song chief' (cá- 'song'); plural càkạbén

chakaben: see Chakabede

Chakwena: cá- 'song'

Chapio: cápìw (?; cá- 'song', pîw- 'death')

ekue 'nest': 'ə́kə̀

eumanune: yə̀yma'úde 'dead infant'

Hakamito: ?

hakuwam 'greetings': 'ak'ûwäˈm—see akuam . . .

Haukabede: hə̀w+kạbéde 'Repletion-chief' (hə̂w-, cf. Taos họwó- 'satiation'; kạbéde, ? cf. Taos kǫ́- 'doctor')

helele: not an Isleta word (l occurs only in words of foreign origin)

hewiav 'thanks': does not look like an Isleta word

Hilili: not an Isleta word; possibly Laguna

hiothliute 'stone old woman' (a place name): híwɫìwte 'stone-woman-at'

Kabewheride: see kabew'iride

kabew'iride: kạbe+hwíride 'Bow Chief' (kạ́be- 'chief', hwír- 'bow', -ide personal ending)

Kapyo: k'ápìw 'clown'

kechu: kécu 'aunt (mother's sister)'

Keipop: kéypäb, a female name (?, pâb 'flower')

Kiama: kíema—cf. kíe- 'stand'

kikawe Weide: kikhà'a+wẽ̂'i wè̩'íde 'our father the spirit' (ki- 'our', khá'a-' father', wè̩'íde 'spirit')

kikewaie Baleyo: kikè+wẽ̂'i p'áɫìw 'our mother Moon Woman' (ki- 'our', ké- 'mother', wẽ̂'i '[the one] who is', p'á- moon, ɫìw- 'woman, wife')

kitu: kitúde 'our community' (ki- 'our', túde 'community, home, pueblo'

296

koa 'throwing stick': khúa

koalakide 'bluejay': k'ùaràkíde (k'ùará- 'magpie', kí- '?', -de)

koat: see koa for possible connection

koatamide: ? khùatamíde (khúa [see koa], ?)

kofanta 'dark blue': k'ùaphừn+tэ̂ name of a kiva group (k'úa- '?', phừn- 'black, dark', tэ̂ 'mark, sign' [?])

kom: kúm 'notched stick' (?)

komnin: kúmnin, ? plural of kúm

Kompor: kùm+phэ̂ar 'notched-stick dance'

Kopishtaiya: a Keresan (Laguna) word

kumeoishi: ? khэm- as in khэ̂mpá (see kumpa)?

kumpa: khэ̂mpá 'war chief' (but Taos has xúm- 'war', which calls for Isleta *khum-; possibly a different stem is involved)

kumpawithlawen: khэ̂mpa+wiłáwin 'war [or 'snake'?] society' (khэ̂mpá [see kumpa], wiłáwin [plural: 'members of ritual] society'

kwarupor 'zigzag dance': kürpэ̂ar—? or same as Quarupör, q.v.

laplaza: Spanish la plaza 'the town, the place'; in Isleta pronounced laplása, and treated as an uninflected word of known foreign flavor (l is not a native Isleta sound)

lifiewah 'medicine water': łìphìe+wár (łí- 'vegetation', phíe- 'root', wár 'medicine')

Mapuride: màphúride 'one who bends' (?); plural, màphúrnin

mapurnin: see Mapuride

nadeke eula 'big bell': nэ̣dӗkì 'эłà

nadeke euree 'small bell': nэ̣dӗki 'ir'э̂'э

nafiechure: nэphìe+c'úri 'Yellow Root' (nэ- noun-class prefix, phíe- 'root', c'úri 'yellow')

nakabato: ?

nam thliu: nàmłìw 'earth woman'

nampe kötö 'Red Earth Hill': nэ̀mphéy+k'э̂tэ'ad (nэ̣m- 'earth', phéy- 'red', k'э̂tэ'ad 'on top')

napeodeke 'dead-strike bell': nэpìw+dӗkéwe 'the death bell is ringing' (pìw- 'death')

natarra dekewa 'chimes': nэtárara dӗkéwè

natosi 'prayer sticks': ? miscopying for natoy or the like—nэtúy 'prayer stick' (nэ- noun-class prefix, túy- 'cane, stick')

natoypor 'prayer stick dance': nэtùy+phэ̂ar (nэ- noun-class prefix, túy- 'cane, stick', phэ̂ar 'dance')

Nawish: not an Isleta word; possibly Laguna

nawah 'mating': nэwâ 'song circle of hunters', literally 'life(-place)'

niuude 'Virgin's baby': ni- '?', 'ừúde 'child'

nu'pöashönti: nừphэ̂ar+šэ̣̂nti 'At the Night-Dance-Going-in' (nừ- 'night', phэ̂ar- 'dance', šэ̣̂n- 'go in', -ti local particle [?]). The Isleta phrase is not a term for 'Christmas Eve dancers', but describes the scene. In 1959 the informant did not recognize šэ̣̂nti as possible in this phrase, and suggested c'э̂atiwe for 'going in'.

pakimu: p'äkímu 'fog, mist' (p'â- 'water')

palimakore: p'э̀łì+makhэ̂ri (p'э̀łí 'salt', ma- '?', khэ̂ri 'circle')

pire 'red': phéy- 'red'

Quarupör: k'ùara+phэ̂ar 'Magpie dance' (k'ùaráde 'magpie')

San Kietiano: for San Gaetano?

Sherida: ? šə̂r'ide personal noun from šə̂r- 'blue, green'

Shichu: šícu, stem-form of šìcúde 'rat, mouse', as name

Shichukabede: šìcu+kạbéde 'rat-chief' (šícu; kạbéde as in càkạbéde—see Chakabede)

shunad: see shunade

shunade 'purification': šunáde '?'

Shure: šúre a name (a kind of bird, "Red Eye")

sumkup: sámkə̀ab 'porcupine shoes' (sám- 'porcupine', kə́ab- shoe, moccasin')

taide 'ritual food offerings': ? téde

teliefpoyan 'the Navaho dead': possibly a miscopying of thliecheyan or the like, in which case see thliachia; or for teliecheyan, see taide, thliachia

thlawashie 'prayer feathers': ?, šíe- 'tied'

thliachia: łíecìe 'food offerings for the dead'

Thliwa: łíwa 'male dancer in full costume; kachina'

Thliwa funide: łìwa+phụ́nide 'black dancer' (łíwa—see thliwa; phụ́nide 'black person')

thliwakompor: łìwakùm+phə́ar (łíwa- 'kachina', kúm- 'notched stick', phə́ar 'dance'

Thliwalpör: this is probably the same as thliwapor, q.v. (l is not a native Isleta sound); if however, l was misheard for r, then we may have wár- 'medicine', and the first element is perhaps łì- 'vegetation'—łìwàr+phə́ar 'plant-medicine dance')

thliwapor 'February dance': łìwa+phə́ar 'kachina dance'

Thliwelepör: possibly the same as Thliwalpör, q.v.

Tochide: thə̀cíde—thə̂- 'day', plus ?

truhi: impossible form for a native Isleta word; cannot be reconstructed into a recognizable form

tuefuni 'Black Cane': túyphụ̀ni (túy 'cane', phụ́nin 'black')

Tuewithlawe 'Cane Chief': tùy+wiłáwi (túy 'cane', wiłáwi[de] 'chief, [member of ritual] society')

uwepo: ? same as uwepör, q.v.

uwepör: 'ùwě+phə́ar ('û- 'child', wě́- 'exist', phə́ar 'dance')

wadinin: see wahtainin

wahtainin 'angels': wàt'áynin—wâ- 'life', t'áynin 'people' (plural)

waiide tainin: wä'íde 'living [person]', t'áynin 'people'

waitinin: see wahtainin

Weide: wè'íde 'spirit', plural wę́nin

wenin: see Weide

wikon: wị́ 'pine', plus ?

wikun 'slow match': see wikon

-withlawe(n): see kumpawithlawen, tuewithlawe

yayu: ?

See page 11, note 15: Taos and Isleta languages are too different for this to be possible so recently; the hypothesis is definitely untenable.

298

REFERENCES

DUMAREST, FATHER NOEL.
  1919. Notes on Cochiti, New Mexico. Translated and edited by Elsie Clews Parsons. Mem. Amer. Anthrop. Assoc., vol. 6, No. 3.

FRENCH, DAVID.
  1948. Factionalism in Isleta Pueblo. Amer. Ethnol. Soc. Monogr. 19. New York.

GOLDFRANK, ESTHER S.
  1927. The social and ceremonial organization of Cochiti. Amer. Anthrop. Assoc. Monogr., No. 33.

LUMMIS, C. F.
  1908. Some strange corners of our country. New York.
  1920. Pueblo Indian folk stories, 1920. (First published in 1891.) New York.

PARSONS, ELSIE CLEWS.
  1932. Isleta, New Mexico. 47th Ann. Rep. Bur. Amer. Ethnol., for 1929–30, pp. 193–466.
  1939. Pueblo Indian religion. Chicago.

STEVENSON, MATILDA COXE.
  1904. The Zuni Indians: Their mythology, estoteric fraternities, and ceremonies. 23d Ann. Rep. Bur. Amer. Ethnol., for 1901–02, pp. 1–634.

STEWARD, JULIAN H.
  1938. Basin-Plateau sociopolitical groups. Bur. Amer. Ethnol. Bull. 120.

TITIEV, MISCHA.
  1944. Old Oraibi. Pap. Peabody Mus. Amer. Archaeol. and Ethnol., Harvard University, vol. 22, No. 1.

WHITE, LESLIE A.
  1935. The Pueblo of Santo Domingo. Mem. Amer. Anthrop. Assoc. No. 43.
  1943. New material from Acoma. Bur. Amer. Ethnol. Bull. 136, Anthrop. Pap. No. 19.

WITTFOGEL, KARL A., and GOLDFRANK, ESTHER S.
  1943. Some aspects of Pueblo mythology and society. Journ. Amer. Folklore, vol. 56, pp. 17–30.

WOODBURY, RICHARD B.
  1954. Prehistoric stone implements of Northeastern Arizona. Pap. Peabody Mus. Amer. Archaeol. and Ethnol., Harvard University, vol. 34, pp. 3–210.